YOUR PRODUCT IS *YOU!*
LEARN HOW TO SELL YOURSELF!

This manual provides a step-by-step comprehensive guide to obtaining the position that is best suited to your talents, your temperament and your training. You'll discover the best techniques to create, organize and implement a job-seeking campaign—*and* get advice on how to avoid the pitfalls and barriers. The self-marketing methods developed here have proved highly successful for many career men and women—and can prove equally successful for you.

The Complete
Résumé Book
& Job-Getter's Guide

Dr. Juvenal L. Angel

A WALLABY BOOK
Published by Pocket Books
New York

A Wallaby Book published by
POCKET BOOKS, a division of Simon & Schuster, Inc.
1230 Avenue of the Americas, New York, N.Y. 10020

ISBN: 0-671-54638-4

Originally published as a Pocket Book

First Wallaby Books printing January, 1985

10 9 8 7 6 5 4 3 2 1

WALLABY and colophon are registered trademarks
of Simon & Schuster, Inc.

Printed in the U.S.A.

Contents

vi

Foreword

This book is aptly named. It is much more than a collection of sample résumés, varied and comprehensive as these are. It is a book that will show you, the job-seeker, exactly how to go about finding the job you want—a job that is in accord with your educational background, your experience, your special talents, your personal interests and your ambition.

Under today's classification, you have four types of model résumés to choose from:

> The Basic Résumé
> The Chronological Résumé
> The Functional Résumé
> The Modern Analytical Résumé

As to the type of résumé you will choose to use in your job search, that depends on you, and how you regard your occupation in relation to the available opportunities in the job market. Whichever résumé you choose to use in your job search, there are abundant samples of each in this book.

The résumé as a means of communication is one of the most vital of all instruments for making a connection. Top copywriters who may be adept at writing copy to promote anything from undeveloped arid land to collapsible cooking utensils suddenly become nonproductive when obliged to write a résumé that will interest the prospective employer and lead to an interview. Why? Because most of us lack the professional know-how to write a good résumé.

It is necessary to realize that a résumé is neither an autobiography nor a memoir. It is a personal advertisement, and the facts it presents must emphasize your accomplishments and abilities. Its purpose is to get you an interview.

Unfortunately, most people are inexperienced in the technique of selling. And since only about 30 percent of our population is engaged in sales work, it is not to be wondered that most of us are unaware of the four most important sales aids. These are

Total objectivity in regard to work and
    accomplishments
Sources from which to expect employment of the
    right kind
Methods of contacting these right sources
The ability to do a selling job at the interview

This manual provides a step-by-step, comprehensive guide to obtaining the position that is best suited to your talents, your temperament and your training. The self-marketing methods suggested here have proved highly successful and should prove equally successful for you. The advice offered for developing, organizing and implementing a job-seeking campaign is combined with advice on how to avoid pitfalls and barriers.

The use of the masculine pronoun in this book is intended to refer to both male and female gender.

The author hopes that the reader, in trying to evaluate himself in relation to his own job potential, will find the techniques and résumés presented here a source of help and inspiration.

Special thanks are due to Fay Lebow, for her constructive criticism in the preparation of the material; and thanks also to Gloria C. Sainz, June L. Aulick, Margaret Raymond, James H. Bradley and Sara Gonzalez for their very much appreciated help.

J. L. Angel
New York, N.Y.

PART 1

Résumé
Fundamentals

Going After
and Getting a Job

Finding a job that provides a good living requires a knowledge of where to look for openings and the ability to present your qualifications effectively.

Normal turnover in the employment market creates opportunities at every level. New positions become available through technological changes and the expansion and development of new industries. Many multinational firms are expanding their operations and facilities, thus increasing their need for people in a variety of occupations.

Determining Your Objective

Let us assume that you have a general idea of the career you wish to pursue. You have devoted your time—from one to six or more years—specializing in subjects related to the vocation you have chosen, or gaining experience. You have acquired the necessary skills and the basic knowledge of international traffic, market analysis and related subjects; and you have familiarized yourself with many of the diplomatic techniques required for the foreign-operations executive. You have learned the principles of advertising and editing in order to pursue a career in public relations or technical writing. Or you know the various employment procedures, the problems of labor relations, and the systems of job-evaluation necessary to the specialist in personnel management. Perhaps you have attended a school of engineering, of scientific management, of design or of nursing.

It is advisable to find out as much as possible about the field you have chosen. Having done this you can ask yourself: Where are the best opportunities? What phases of the work am I best qualified for?

There are a number of ways in which the information can be obtained: You can learn from actual experience. You can talk to faculty members or occupational consultants who are familiar with your vocational interests. You can consult a placement director who, being in constant touch with employment opportunities, may be able to advise you as to the type of opening best suited to your present ability and experience. Or you can talk to persons who are already doing similar work—those who, as graduates, have preceded you, or those who have already attained eminence in the field. Be sure to check your library for books on the particular subject that interests you.

Your research will give you an overall idea of the opportunities that are available in your field. It will not, however, tell you just what to do. This you must determine for yourself.

It is wise to set a long-term goal. Know what you eventually hope to become, and strive in all possible ways toward that goal. You must realize that it is only in rare instances that your first job will provide all the challenge, inspiration and satisfaction that you hope to attain. It will, however, offer experience that may later be used to good advantage in securing a position that is in accord with your ideal.

If you are among those who, possessing many interests and general abilities, can't decide how to use them to best advantage, aptitude tests or personal interviews with experts can help you. But do not allow yourself to be lured into paying large sums of money for aptitude tests before you have assured yourself that the organization providing the tests, such as the National Vocational Guidance Association, has an approved reputation.

If you have access to business or professional leaders who understand your shortcomings as well as your strong points, by all means consult them. Perhaps the position you want requires additional training, such as a degree or some specialized courses. It is for you to decide the road to follow: Should you accept another position and attend night school, or would it be better to take a correspondence course? Should you enroll in a school or college that offers a cooperative plan under which you can study part-time and work part-time? Whatever you decide, see to it that you master the fundamentals required for the work you want to do. It is very difficult to find employment when you are only partly trained for the work you want to do.

While it is advisable in many instances to specialize (and specialization usually pays good financial dividends), it is wise to have some other vocational abilities, as a sort of backlog, in case of an economic slump or depression. For example, a person who can type or take dictation might be able to find a job on that basis alone when conditions are not favorable for a job as a foreign-trade specialist or a public-relations consultant.

In summary: Decide what you really want to do by means of acquiring as much information as you can about your particular job interest. Set an eventual goal and work toward that goal. At the same time, be prepared for an adverse situation by developing different skills on which you can rely in an emergency.

Selling Yourself (as Well as Your Abilities)

Applying for a position can be compared with selling merchandise. In the former you are attempting to sell yourself—your skills and abilities; and you are trying to convince an employer that by hiring you he will make a good investment. In order to sell yourself, however, you need to know yourself to the extent that you can answer promptly and directly any question that you may be asked at an interview.

The first step, then, in a job-hunting campaign is to make up a personal inventory of your assets. This can be done either by memorizing your inventory or by having it in written form. The important thing is to have all pertinent data handy when needed. Not all employers will be interested in the same information about you. Their methods can be as varied as their personalities. What they will want to know depends largely on their experience with other prospective employees.

One employer will regard education as the principal criterion upon which to base a decision and will question you about the courses you have taken, the marks you received and your general interest in school work. Another employer may feel that your previous experience and work record, together with a list of former employers and the kind of work you did, are of more importance. A third may take the view that extracurricular activities and hobbies reveal more about an applicant than any other information and will ask more questions about these. And still another may want to know more about family background and personality.

Since you cannot know until you are at the actual interview what will be required of you, it is best to be prepared with answers to different kinds of questions. It can make the difference between success or failure in securing a position.

Review your assets and liabilities for the work you would like and can do. Remember that your best chance for success is when you select the job that is right for you. Following are some good tips for a systematic campaign for getting and holding a position:

(1) Take stock of yourself.
(2) Prepare an effective résumé or job summary.
(3) Consider job requirements and how well you can meet them.
(4) Know where to look for a position.
(5) Write a good covering letter.
(6) Be prepared for the interview.

Personal Characteristics

Although specialized knowledge and skill are a "must" in applying for some jobs, many personnel experts place 75 to 85 percent of the emphasis on such qualifications as appearance, character, intelligence, dependability and attitude, when considering a new applicant. Experience is of course valuable, but it cannot substitute for such personal characteristics as honesty, the ability to work and get along with others, resourcefulness and initiative. There are many people who are experts at their chosen occupations, who fail to advance because they lack one or more of these personal qualities. Employers are very much interested in those who possess these qualities.

Self-Appraisal of Your Potential

Employers are likely to be skeptical about those who claim to be superior or special. A person who claims he can do "anything" may prejudice a prospective employer adversely. Such an employer wants to know exactly what you can do and how you can fit into the organization.

In evaluating yourself, therefore, it might be an idea to make a detailed, realistic inventory of your qualifications, interests, and even your limitations. You might commit these to memory or writing in the form of some simple, direct questions which you can answer when asked. These are

(1) What jobs have you held previously?
(2) What did you like and dislike about them?
(3) What specific skills do you possess? (For example, the extent of your technical background.)
(4) What has been your education? How does it qualify you for a particular job?
(5) What are your interests?
(6) Have you any special talents or aptitudes? (For example, in music, painting, writing, sports.)
(7) What physical condition would limit you in any way?
(8) What kind of job do you really want?

More and more organizations are checking high school records, former teachers and personal references, not only for scholastic information or previous work experience, but for such personal items as alertness, good manners, ability to get along with others, punctuality, respect for authority and leadership qualities.

Except in certain instances, specialized skills and prior experience are secondary in considering a new applicant for a job. Orientation periods, on-the-job training programs and apprenticeships are some of the ways in which many businesses and industries provide opportunities for new employees to acquire skills and experience.

Practically all jobs make some physical demands, so that most companies require candidates to pass a physical examination. This results in the certainty that an employee will be placed in a job that is in line with his or her physical capacities. Good health is essential to good work performance, so make sure that you can meet the physical requirements of the job you seek.

Personal appearance is important. It is a factor stressed by most employers when considering an applicant. Neatness, cleanliness, good manners and a friendly, cooperative disposition make for a pleasant and presentable personality. The disheveled or "not-quite-put-together" look gives employers a first impression of sloppiness or irresponsibility. They want dignified and responsible people in their businesses and will expect these qualities to be reflected in the appearance and actions of all employees. Employers respect young men and women who show a sense of propriety and good taste in dress and bearing.

2

Everyone Needs a Self-Appraisal Record

Your Occupational Inventory

Before you start preparing your résumé, the first and most important step is to make up a personal occupational work sheet. The facts you set down in your work sheet are those you will consider and reconsider in the light of the kind of job you are seeking and the field you wish to enter. This is why, in preparing your work sheet, you are really providing yourself with a reliable tool to use in writing your final résumé.

Your occupational inventory can be regarded as a personal biography that places emphasis on your employment history. The information on your work sheet or occupational inventory includes your name and address, your education, the positions you have held in the past, the job you now hold and what you would like to do in the future.

It will serve you in the same way that an account work sheet serves an accountant, who has before himself a concentrated résumé of the figures he needs to prepare a balance sheet and other financial statements.

11

If your occupational work sheet is well organized, you can easily prepare your résumé, or write a well-expressed letter about your work experience.

Perhaps you are one of those who consider the preparation of an occupational work sheet a waste of time. You may be right—if you change jobs once or twice in your lifetime and are currently employed in a job where you are happy and which you do not intend to leave. Otherwise, to be ready for any opportunity that may come along at any time, you must have your occupational inventory prepared and easily available. Regardless of the kind of job, you are going to be asked for some specific information—and this is what your occupational inventory contains and what it is for.

Sample of a Typical Occupational Inventory

The occupational inventory that follows contains all the sections you will need. It is a sample of an actual occupational inventory. Remember that in preparing your final résumé you do not have to include all the facts included in your work sheet. It is important that you include only what is directly pertinent to your field of interest, but state this clearly so that you will be understood.

Following is a list that is intended to provide all possible entries for the preparation of your work sheet or occupational inventory:

(1) Name and Address
Start by writing your name and address on one side of the sheet, and your telephone number on the other. Leave one blank line between your name and your address, allowing your name to stand out. You may type this flush left on the sheet, or indented somewhat.

(2) Personal Data

The general tendency is to give personal data on one line after the name and address. Some personnel and employment managers find that this rather standard information (marital status, height, weight, health) limits their knowledge of you. Many prefer more extensive facts at the end of the résumé, while others pass over this data because they attach more importance to your experience, education and abilities. Where to place this is optional and the choice is yours; however, we recommend that you use the end of the résumé.

(3) Summary of Experience

In about fifty words, summarize the duties and responsibilities in the different positions you have held up to the present. Show what kind of worker you are. Be brief and to the point. Save the time of the person who will read your résumé.

(4) Occupational Objective

This should be a clearly worded statement of the field in which you want to work. It is most important that you express yourself exactly here, or else you might find yourself in a position that fits your qualifications but does not use your abilities completely. This statement should also tell the reader of your résumé that you are not looking for just anything that might come along. Your overall objective should be stated in general terms, but the specific points you wish to make should be worded precisely.

(5) Experience Record (Highlights)

(a) Give the names and addresses of companies for which you worked, in reverse chronological order.

(b) In the left-hand margin, list the length of time you worked in each place.

(c) Give the titles of your positions, if any. Underline these and write a general description of each company.

(d) In listing your former positions, give as much information as possible. For the final draft of your résumé you can extract the more pertinent information.

(6) Summer and Part-Time Employment

If you have held a part-time or summer job that added to your experience and ability in the field of your interest, include this important information. State the name of the company, the year(s), and the work you performed.

(7) Education

Clearly detailed information about your education is most useful and important. Begin with your most advanced degree; if you have a master's, name the field of the degree, the school, its address, the year, your major subject and any pertinent facts connected with attaining the degree, especially the titles and publication dates, if any, of your thesis or dissertation.

(8) Military Service

Whether in time of peace or war, your military standing must be stated; this is a point almost always questioned by employment or personnel managers. Also, if your specialty in the service is directly connected to your present field of endeavor, give the facts about that work.

14

(9) Professional Licenses

If you work in a field that requires licenses from either local, state or federal authorities, state the kind(s) you have.

(10) Professional Affiliations

Information about memberships in professional societies, including college fraternities, should be presented here. State any special function, duty, title or administrative post you may hold (or have held), and whether you are an active, honorary or professional member.

(11) Literary Accomplishments

State the titles, publishers and dates of printing of all articles, papers, theses or books you have written. Some employers like their employees to have what is called literary "visibility."

(12) Early Background

Employers generally want this information because it is part of the story of the whole person. This section tells the prospective employer part of your history as a child, and some of the forces that shaped you, especially environment, early education and first after-school jobs.

(13) Personal Interests

Here is where you list the hobbies, pastimes and interests that you enjoy and practice in your free time. Emphasize those directly connected with your field of interest. Also include any clubs or societies to which you belong that are related to your hobby. Questions on personal interests are found on virtually all application blanks and included in most interviews.

(14) Outside Activities

This should include the names of all political, social, church, civic and community organizations in which you participate actively. This information also tells the employment or personnel manager something about you outside of your work history.

(15) Knowledge of Foreign Languages

Many companies extending their interests abroad through exports, foreign investments and overseas branches have an increasing demand for employees who speak languages other than English fluently. List those languages you can speak well, but do not assume that high school and college courses make a complete education. Either you know a language fluently, or you do not. Personnel interviewers will almost certainly have you take a test in the foreign tongue, and a failure in this test is held against you. Therefore, honesty is the best policy.

(16) Clerical Skills

Any skill you have in various clerical duties should be entered here. You can never know when such knowledge will influence a final decision in your favor. While some employers are not interested in your ability with clerical tasks, there are just as many who are.

(17) Personal Data

This is the same entry that is generally placed near the beginning of the résumé, but which we recommend at the end.

Date of birth (optional)   Height
Marital status (optional)   Weight
Health   Willing to relocate?
Date of last physical   Will travel?

(18) References

You should list at least three business and three character references here, but be certain you have obtained permission from all of them to use their names. Though your friends, some may not like giving recommendations they have not authorized.

Rather than take the chance of a reference not being able to write a recommendation, or being unwilling to do so, write the letter yourself so that the reference has merely to sign it. Each letter should be different, stressing those good points of yours with which the reference is most familiar.

Make each of these letters short, to the point and honest. If what you write is the truth, you need not hesitate to ask the reference to sign. Explain that you have written it yourself to save time, and leave a copy.

Your Résumé as a Working Passport

A practical way to handle all the details you've gathered in your self-analysis is to present a résumé, personally or by mail, to potential employers. It should be perfectly typed on a good grade of bond paper, in clear analytical, functional or chronological form.

Your background, education and experience determine the order of the facts in your résumé. Spotlight the facts that are particularly relevant to the job, subordinating the ones that have little or no bearing. For example, if you are well trained for, but inexperienced in, the job you want, the information about your education should get preferred treatment. Some authorities recommend putting personal data (name, age, marital status and the like) first, where they strike the eye immediately. In this book we recommend that the personal data come after the more vital information about your abilities, education and experience.

In making up your résumé, first check the questions that can be answered from your occupational work sheet; then check over your resulting "raw material" at least three times. You are now ready to type a résumé, organizing the information into the general form of one of the samples. The different kinds of résumés—basic, chronological, functional, modern analytical—are explained in chapters 6, 7, 8 and 9. Remember, the best form for you depends on the specific background you have to offer.

The résumé should be easy to read, and it should be easy to follow graphically. Dates and headings are used to lead the reader. A personnel manager probably reads résumés for several hours each day; if yours is concise and correct, you stand a better chance of having it read and remembered.

Much has been written about the difference between the functional and the chronological résumés—as to which is the better. Of late, the form that is considered the most practical and is most in favor is that which is a combination of both. It is known as the modern analytical résumé.

A résumé can easily be compared to a passport. You think of a passport when you want to travel abroad, but you find that, before the government will issue one to you, you must supply certain information and meet certain health and character requirements.

A good résumé is your most important job-finding tool. It consists of information brought together in your self-analysis. It should be typed neatly on standard 8½-by-11-inch white paper, suitable for reproduction on a copying machine.

In writing your résumé, strive for brevity but don't omit important or essential information. Most person-

18

nel managers say they prefer one- or two-page résumés, but the length of yours will depend on your particular situation. Ten or twenty-five copies of your résumé may be enough if you're seeking a secretarial or clerical job. For specialized work or an executive position, you may need 100 or more copies, which can be reproduced in a number of ways: mimeographed, offset or photocopied. The offset process is the one that is gaining favor today, because it offers a more formal, permanent and elegant appearance, and the cost is usually quite low. Carbon copies should be kept for your file, but they should never be sent to an employer.

Why Not Let the Mails Work for You?

You can let the mails work for you by preparing and circulating your résumé with a short accompanying letter explaining why you are seeking employment with the company addressed. This way you don't need to travel—your résumé will do the looking for you, either close to home or far away. Just decide where you want to work, then distribute your résumé and accompanying letter in that area.

It is suggested that you consult someone in your local public library to help you find the proper directory or other source of names and addresses of prospective employers. Librarians can give you this information without any difficulty, and they are very accommodating.

Prepare a list of likely prospects, and address the envelopes, making sure to include the proper ZIP code number. When your copy has been printed or reproduced in some other way, type the name of the person, firm and address at the top of each letter, sign it at the bottom, and then insert the letter with the résumé in one of the envelopes. Stamp it, drop it in the mailbox, and the postman will do the rest.

Some companies may not have a job to offer you when they receive your résumé and letter. But a company may be impressed with what you have submitted and will, therefore, decide to keep it for future reference. Or it may be that a company may have a job that is not precisely in your field, but that is closely related to it. Hence, if your résumé does not result in immediate employment, it may be the means of a future connection. Many personnel executives keep résumés that appeal to them on file for long periods of time.

3

Your Own
Job Potential

An Overall View of the Job–Manpower Relationship

In the never-ending flux of the economy, new kinds of jobs are constantly being created, while the demand for others abates. This presents a difficult problem to workers who need to match their abilities and interests with the changing occupational choices that confront them. The changing job market gives rise to such questions as the following: What fields look promising for employment opportunities? What education and training are required to undertake particular jobs? How do earnings in certain occupations compare with earnings in other occupations that require similar training? What types of employers provide which kinds of jobs? Does employment in a particular job mean steady, year-round work, or is the job seasonal or affected by minor swings in economic activity?

The answers to these questions change as the economy changes and expands. New goods, services, improved methods of production and changes in living standards, life styles and government policies are continually affecting the job market. This section explores the changes in our industrial and economic pattern and how they affect the employment situation as regards specific occupations. It discusses the implications of these changes for career education, vocational training, the experience needed and job characteristics.

The following groups of workers in the labor force will, in the immediate future, be most affected by the changes in the economy and the resulting changes in job requirements: black workers, younger workers and women.

Nonwhite workers are concentrated disproportionately in less-skilled occupations that have higher-than-average unemployment rates. The need for these occupations is not expected to grow as rapidly as the need for more-skilled occupations. If nonwhites do not gain access to white-collar and skilled jobs at a faster rate than heretofore, they will continue to have serious unemployment problems.

Young workers, another group that is experiencing high unemployment, are also part of the slower-growing, less-skilled occupations. The number of young workers will increase more rapidly in the next decade than the labor force as a whole. To deal with the problem of high unemployment among the young, industry may have to lower the minimum hiring age in certain occupations, use younger workers as aides or assistants to the mature and experienced workers or promote young workers at a faster rate to more-skilled jobs.

Women are concentrated in the rapidly growing white-collar occupations. If their share of jobs in various occupations remains unchanged, their employment problems will be no more serious than those they now have. However, men are seriously and increasingly competing for some of the occupations that were traditionally held by women. Among these are teaching, social work, library work and similar white-collar jobs. If this trend continues, more women workers may have to seek employment in other fields.

Our current technologically oriented society generates technological changes that strongly affect occupational requirements. However, many factors other than technological developments influence the employment situation in specific occupations. These factors include the different rate of employment growth among different industries, population rise and fall, government expenditures and institutional changes. Technology is inextricably interwoven with these factors and its impact cannot be separated from them.

One of the major manifestations of occupational changes is the growth in population and its changing age distribution. A rapid increase in population can bring a sharp rise in the demand for goods and services and result in more employment in industry. As the population grows there is a concomitant increase in production of such items as food, clothing, housing—also leading to more employment. A growing population will also require more services and a rise in the demand for such workers as barbers, cosmetologists, lawyers, bankers and doctors. And with an increase in urbanization, there is need for more state and local government employees, including such workers as firemen and policemen.

The changes in age distribution also play a major role in influencing the occupations that are available. A greater number of teachers, for example, is needed for the increase in the number of school-age children. Similarly, the increase in the number of older persons

23

results in greater demand for medical and paramedical personnel.

Government policy as regards federal, state and local expenditures plays a significant role in determining the occupational employment composition. Expenditures for education, for example, generate the need for more teachers, as well as for construction workers, and still other personnel to maintain and administer schools. Occupations such as social work, medicine, nursing, and highway engineering are also affected by the extent and direction of government spending.

The varying rates of employment growth among different industries are among the most important elements that determine occupational distribution in the United States. As an example, we can note that the growth in white-collar workers is the result of the more-than-average growth in industries that need them. Among these industries are state and local government, finance, insurance, real estate and business and professional services. A much slower rate of growth prevails in such industries as mining, manufacturing and transportation, which employ fewer white-collar workers.

The recent rise in employment in the manufacturing and construction industries is a manifestation of growth in the national economy. As a corollary to this growth in the manufacturing and construction industries, there has been for half a decade a sharp downward trend for blue-collar workers.

Collective bargaining and the relationship between labor and management are part of the occupational pattern of industry. In the railroad, shipping and newspaper industries, unions have encouraged the maintenance of occupational skills. And union-management decisions are likely to have a marked effect on the occupational pattern of the economy as a whole.

Scarcities and surpluses also affect occupations.

They provide management with the opportunity to maneuver jobs to match, to some degree, the available supply of workers. As an example, when engineers are in short supply, additional technicians are hired to perform certain routine engineering jobs. In other instances, a production process may be adjusted to employ a combination of labor skills that are different from those in short supply.

Organizational changes and improvements in managerial practices also influence the growth rate of occupations. Mergers, acquisitions and streamlining of administrative procedures have their effect on middle-management jobs. More-liberal tax terms, lower corporate tax rates and new depreciation guidelines affect occupations, in that they can increase the profitability of new machinery and equipment.

Important Job-Finding Areas

Administration and Management are concerned with running businesses and other organizations. Some administrators supervise, plan operations and establish policy. Others provide assistance to management through personnel specialists who recruit and hire staff members and handle labor relations. The success or failure of an organization depends to a large extent on the way administrators do their jobs.

Nearly all positions at this level require a college degree, although employers have different ideas relating to specific areas of study that they prefer. Some employers seek business administration or liberal arts graduates; others want a technical background, such as in engineering or the sciences.

Agriculture in both the professional and commercial branches offers unusual opportunities to those who are

25

suitably equipped. Let us look at commercial farming. While the number of farms has declined in the past decade from 7 million to less than 5½ million, the value of farm products has jumped from $18 billion to $22 billion a year. Farm production and farm income have gone up steadily in the past decade because of the use of highly complex and efficient farm equipment, and because of better seed, feed, fertilizer and livestock. Farming today is more and more an industrial enterprise.

Professional agriculture, which includes the various applied agricultural sciences, has grown steadily in the past decade. It shows promise of increasing importance in the future, as greater emphasis is placed on research to improve methods and increase productivity.

Aircraft, of which there are a number of different kinds, include missiles and spacecraft. They all have the same basic components: a frame to hold and support the vehicle, an engine to propel it and a guidance and control system. Missiles and spacecraft reach into space at speeds many times that of sound, while conventional aircraft fly in the atmosphere of the earth at slower speeds. Missiles are powered by either jet or rocket engines; spacecraft are rocket-powered. Conventional aircraft are powered by piston, jet or rocket engines.

Types of aircraft vary from small planes for business or personal use that do not cost much more than an automobile, to multimillion-dollar jumbo transports and supersonic fighters manufactured for military use.

Missiles are chiefly for military purposes. They generally carry destructive warheads. Some, such as those that support ground troops and defend against low-flying enemy aircraft, are capable of traveling only limited distances. Others have intercontinental ranges of 7,000 miles or more.

Banking, Finance, Insurance and Real Estate offer services to nearly every individual and organization. Financial institutions (banks, savings and loan companies, consumer and credit organizations) offer services ranging from checking and savings accounts to the handling of stock and bond transactions. Insurance firms provide protection against losses caused by fire, accident, sickness and death. Real estate organizations serve as agents in the sale or rental of buildings and property and often manage large offices and apartments.

Finance, insurance, and real estate firms are a major source of job opportunities for women, who make up over half of the industry's work force, ranging from about 35 percent in real estate to over 60 percent in banking.

Banks have been described as "department stores of finance" because they offer a variety of services ranging from individual checking accounts to letters of credit for financing world trade. Banks safeguard money and valuables, administer trusts and personal estates, and lend money to businesses and to educational, religious and other organizations. They also lend money for the purchase of homes, automobiles and household items, and to cover unexpected financial needs. Banks continually strive to serve their customers' needs. In recent years, for example, they have offered revolving-check credit plans, charge cards, accounting and billing services and money-management counseling.

Bench-Work Occupations are concerned with the specialized fine work required on many small objects and materials. The work is usually done on a worktable or conveyor. The worker uses hands, hand tools and bench machines to find, paint, sew, put together, inspect or repair a product. The product might be a musical instrument, an article of clothing or jewelry, or one of a number of different items. Beginning workers usually are assigned to a particular repetitive step in the production process. Beginners who acquire experience can move up to more difficult work that may require reading blueprints to meet standards of size and measurement.

Communications offer expanding opportunities for employment. The ability to express oneself by means of the written and spoken word, to understand and interpret information and to transmit that understanding to others is required. Occupations in this field include interpreting, technical writing, journalism, radio and television newscasting, publicity and public relations.

Construction is an industry that touches almost every aspect of our daily lives. The houses and apartments in which we live, the factories, offices and schools where we work, the roads for transporting manufactured and agricultural products, and on which people travel, are products of this important industry. It is concerned not only with new construction projects, but also with additions, alterations and repairs to existing structures.

Extracting Industries are involved with the mining and petroleum industries, which provide most of the basic raw materials and energy sources for our industrial and consumer use. Metal mines provide iron, copper, gold and other products. Quarrying and other nonmetal activities yield limestone and gravel for schools, offices, homes and highways. Few products from mines reach the consumer in their natural state. Nearly all require further processing.

Most of the energy for industrial and personal use that we require comes from oil, gas and coal. Petroleum is one of the fuels formed by the decay of living matter.

It is extracted mainly in the form of crude oil and natural gas. Those engaged in this area find oil and gas and bring them to the surface of the earth for conversion into usable products. Gas processing involves removing water, sulfur compounds and other impurities from natural gas and separating liquid gases such as ethanol and propane.

Crude-oil and natural-gas production covers three broad fields: exploration, drilling and the operation and maintenance of wells. Firms that specialize in these activities under contract to oil companies employ almost half of all workers in petroleum production. Major oil companies employ most of the remainder. Since oil and gas are difficult to find, exploration and drilling are key activities in the petroleum industry.

Farming, Forestry, Fishing Occupations include the production of food and fibers. Off-farm occupations stem from the need for agricultural products, the use of agricultural resources, horticulture and the products of our forests. Some of the occupations in this category are farmhand, farm-equipment operator, cowpuncher, fisherman, fire lookout, nursery worker, gamekeeper and forester aide. High school graduates will find good beginning opportunities in both farm and off-farm fields.

Industrial Production or Manufacturing is a key activity of our nation's economy. Products of manufacturing range from simple plastic toys to intricate electronic computers, and from miniature electronic components to gigantic aircraft carriers. Manufacturing involves many diverse processes. Men and women process foods and chemicals, print books and newspapers, spin and weave textiles, make clothing and shoes and produce thousands of other articles for our personal and national needs.

Millions of people who work in industrial production help to ensure the growth and smooth operation of our economy. Skilled and semiskilled workers are employed mainly in factories. Machinists and machine-tool operators shape metal to precise sizes. Assemblers put together automobiles, television sets, and hundreds of other products. Inspectors examine and test products to assure quality. Printing craftsmen operate various types of machinery used to print newspapers, books and other publications. Some factory workers are not directly involved in the production process, but support it in other ways. Stationary engineers, for example, operate boilers and other equipment. Millwrights move and install heavy industrial machinery. Power-truck operators move materials within a plant.

Industrial workers are also employed outside of plants in a variety of occupations. Automobile painters, for instance, restore the finish on old and damaged cars. Photographic laboratory technicians develop film and make prints and slides.

Semiskilled workers, such as assemblers and power-truck operators, ordinarily need only brief on-the-job training. Skilled workers, such as stationary engineers and machinists, require considerable training to qualify for their jobs. Many learn their trades on the job, but training authorities recommend completion of three- or four-year apprenticeship programs as the best way to acquire skill in a trade.

Machine-Trades Occupations are concerned with installing, setting up, running, keeping up and repairing machines and mechanical equipment used to make parts out of materials such as metals, paper, wood and stone. Most jobs in this category require skills and judgment that can be gained only through training and experience. Therefore, apprenticeships or helpers' jobs are the best way to get into most machine-trades occupations.

Office Occupations require workers to perform a wide variety of tasks associated with a business and other kinds of organizations. Clerical workers, secretaries and typists maintain files, take dictation, type and operate office machines. Professional and technical workers give legal advice, prepare and analyze financial reports, design computer systems and arrange bank loans.

Office work attracts and employs people from widely different educational backgrounds. Some jobs can be entered with only a high school education; others, however, may require a college degree.

Some types of clerical work are detailed and repetitive. A great many office workers, however, apply their skills to solving problems and devising ways to improve services and to make operations more efficient. Apart from certain special skills office workers possess, they need to exercise judgment and must have the ability to communicate their ideas to others.

Paramedical Occupations are those that require working in and around private and public hospitals; serving individuals in institutions, in business and other establishments; and rendering services that are required by crime, fire, accidents, riots, acts of war, etc. A number of paramedical jobs require special training and licensing.

Processing Occupations are concerned with treating, mixing, compounding and refining materials and products such as metals, foods, wood products and chemicals. Jobs typically involve working with vats, stills, ovens, furnaces, mixing machines, crushers, grinders and similar equipment. A large number of beginning opportunities for technicians occur in processing occupations.

Programming and Computing satisfy data-processing needs that have increased very rapidly over the past decade. Business organizations have become

31

more complex as scientific and technical knowledge has expanded. The computer has enabled us to keep pace with the increasing need for more direct access to information. Workers in computer and related occupations prepare data in the form necessary for machine processing; they operate computer consoles and various related equipment and analyze and interpret the machine's output.

Most computer careers require specialized training that varies in content and length of time. While there are no universal educational requirements for systems analysts and programmers, a college degree is increasingly important, especially for work in scientific and technical systems. Computer operators usually need at least a high school education. However, training and experience are considered more important than formal education.

All computer jobs, including those that require a college education, stress the importance of learning on the job. While this is the primary source of training, college graduates in computer science may also spend a year or more working on a system to learn how it functions.

In addition to technical knowledge and skill, computer personnel need good power of concentration and should enjoy detail work. Those who operate equipment—keypunch or console operators—must have manual dexterity and some mechanical aptitude. Although programmers and systems analysts seldom run computer equipment, they also need mechanical ability to trace the source of data-processing errors.

Sales Occupations offer career opportunities for those who have completed high school as well as for college graduates, for those who wish to travel and those who do not wish to travel, and for salaried workers as well as for those who prefer to be in business for themselves.

32

Outside of retail selling, most sales persons are men. A large number are automobile salesmen, automobile-parts countermen, gasoline-service attendants and routemen. Mostly, sales jobs require selling for manufacturers, service firms, wholesalers and retailers.

Space Exploration comprises manned and unmanned operations, communication by Telstar, work in the oceans' depths and the use of automated, petrochemical and similar complex manufacturing and processing systems, as well as biomedical research. The acquisition of knowledge in these and other areas of applied science would be impossible without the use of sensitive instruments that provide the means for exact measurements and control, and information as to storage and retrieval. This rapidly growing and increasingly important area of applied science is broadly termed instrumentation.

Although some of the principles of instrumentation and automatic control have been known for almost 200 years, it is only within the last thirty years that much of the theory, and the advanced techniques used in systems analyses, have been developed. The serious demand for the skills needed in measurement and the use of control equipment has resulted in the stepped-up development of new methods and devices in instrumentation. New industries, new applications and the development of many facets of physics have created and are continuing to create new methods of instrumentation and control.

The availability of analog and digital computers, the development of minutely accurate position sensors, and the techniques for storing vast quantities of information for easy retrieval are creating a revolution in the business-machines industry and in the machine-tool field, and are promoting new skills in industries that require closed-loop control systems to provide automatic process or systems control.

Adequate training of engineers, scientists and supporting technical personnel is an increasing problem. Highly qualified instrumentation personnel must be trained in not one but several of the traditional scientific or engineering disciplines. They must combine both mechanical and electronic engineering with theoretical and applied physics in order to develop the devices and concepts of instrumentation.

Structural-Work Occupations include those required to build and keep up structural parts used in buildings, bridges, motor vehicles, etc. Factory production-line jobs, as well as those jobs done outside of factories or shops, belong in this category. Workers use hand and portable power tools. They work with wood, metal, concrete, glass, clay and other materials. Since most of these occupations require a knowledge of the materials being used, beginners will find apprenticeships and helpers' jobs a good way to enter the structural-work occupations.

Miscellaneous Occupations are those that do not fit into any of the particular categories referred to. These occupations may include transportation services, packaging materials and storing items in warehouses, production and motion-picture services, mining and logging, graphic-art work, and a great many other activities.

4

The Development
of Your Résumé

The Problem of Preparing Your Résumé

Preparing your résumé may not seem to be a problem. And yet it is just that—a problem made up of doubts about yourself, and about the kind of person who will read your résumé, the conditions under which it will be read and the overall business situation which might affect your job search. Then, too, though you may have confidence in your qualifications for a job, you might feel less confident about your ability to present them clearly enough to attract the attention of a prospective employer. You might even, in the midst of your self-doubts, consider the idea of seeking professional advice to prepare your résumé.

Well, rest assured and abandon your self-doubts. If you possess the qualifications for the job you are seeking and are willing to study the model résumés in this book, you will, as a matter of course, acquire the ability to write a very good résumé.

After all, what is a résumé? It is not an autobiography, nor is it a personal memoir. Plainly defined, it is a record of your working life past and present as related to your future goals and expectations and as measured by your ambition. It is a sort of self-advertisement of these, presenting the facts about your accomplishments and abilities, and its purpose is to open the door of a job for you with a prospective employer.

Your first step, therefore, and the easiest way to begin, is to pick up a model that suits you from the "Guide to Types of Résumés for More than 400 Leading Occupations" (chapter 5). But, before you do this, it is suggested that you familiarize yourself with the basic principles of what a good résumé in your category should include. These are discussed in the following four chapters, one for each kind of résumé.

The Résumé That Expresses You

It is you who will have to decide whether you want to write an analytical, functional, chronological or basic résumé. These four types are presented in this book to help you choose. Whichever you choose, you will need to present all the facts about your qualifications and experience for your prospective employer to consider, with a view to your possible employment.

Your résumé may be submitted to public and private employment agencies, to college and university placement offices or to specialized executives within a particular company. Of course you know that your résumé will be considered in accordance with the Fair Employment Practice Law. If you feel that information as to your age, race, color, religion or national origin may be useful to an employer, you may include this information; you are under no obligation, according to law, to do so.

Remember that your résumé is your advertisement. It summarizes what you have to offer an employer for a particular position. It must interest the person who is going to buy your knowledge, experience, skill, ambition, creativity. The purpose of your résumé is to get you an invitation to be interviewed or to submit a formal application.

The person or persons who read your résumé are busy, so make it brief. One or two pages are sufficient, or three if absolutely necessary. In presenting the facts about yourself, make every word carry full meaning. Be informative and to the point. Summarize your abilities as related to selected areas that are directly connected to the kind of work you do. In your attempt to be brief, do not, however, fall into the trap of making your statements so terse that they fail to give the intended information.

Begin each statement with the past-tense verb form. You might, for instance, say: "*Directed* and *supervised* applied research in personnel administration," or "*Administered* entire enlisted training program."

Bear in mind that your résumé is your passport to employment. Be concise and yet complete. Don't hesitate to relate your personal qualifications and objectives to the position you seek. Sell yourself, your abilities and your attitudes to your prospective employer.

Include all the facts that are related to the necessary information. Organize and present your data as briefly and clearly as you can to take full advantage of the suggested résumé pattern. Put yourself in the place of an interviewer who has to read many résumés and see many applicants each day, and your need to be brief, concise and well organized will become clear to you.

Be careful, however, not to overreach the actual facts about yourself. If you do this you may not be able to support your statements in a face-to-face interview. You must resist the temptation to make your résumé do more for you than it can.

Choose the Model Résumé That Fits You

Following one of the model résumés in this book will help you write your own résumé. Pattern yours after the one that does the most for you and your situation. Be sure that you follow the sample in appearance and length and organization when preparing yours.

Few, if any, applicants succeed in obtaining a personal interview unless they have a satisfactory résumé. You may have excellent qualifications and worthwhile experience, but if you cannot present these clearly and concisely to a prospective employer, you have little chance of being interviewed. You need the appearance of prestige for your profession or occupation.

Many firms keep files of possible applicants for their future needs in what is known as their Office of Human Resources, or their Personnel Department. These files relate to all sorts of jobs: salesmen, controllers, accountants, skilled and unskilled workers; and they are consulted when jobs in the particular categories are available.

Executives are well aware that qualified employees are not always easy to find. They also know that many apply for positions without possessing the necessary qualifications. Do not follow the old idea that all you need is an opportunity. Make certain that you have the necessary background and experience for the position you seek, and then present these in detail in your résumé. Let your résumé open the door to the job you want.

Decide Whether Your Résumé Will Be Long or Short

There are no definite rules as to how long a résumé should be. If your history is short because your education or experience is limited, or for some other personal reason, one page will suffice. But when you have to present a lengthy history of background, experience and potential, you can use either two or three pages—never more than three. Employers seldom have the time to read more than three pages, and if you write more the reader may miss some information while trying to cover all you have included.

In short, your résumé should be long enough to tell the prospective employer all that he should know, and short enough to avoid trivia. The generally accepted average is one page for applicants with little experience—such as recent college graduates—two pages for applicants with up to ten years' experience, and three pages for professional people and executives, who usually have long years of experience.

General Notes for an Effective Résumé

(1) The samples of résumés for various job areas included in this chapter are for your guidance. Study them carefully and follow the format in preparing your own. They are all samples of four leading résumés, the type used by better placement and personnel services. Include all functions related to your experience and the job areas in which you are interested.

(2) Always use good quality paper for résumés, at least 50 percent rag bond, preferably the standard 8½-by-11-inch size. Odd sizes—legal paper, for instance—are difficult to handle and file. Send a good

Multilith or mimeograph copy to prospective employers, references, friends or other business contacts.

(3) Place your full name, in capitals, at the top center of each page. Omit your present status, since this can be included in any covering letter you may send out.

(4) If your résumé is more than one page long, type "Page 1 of 2 (or 3)" at the bottom of the first page. At the bottom of page 2, type "Page 2 of 2 (or 3)." Do the same for page 3. The employer can then know the length of your résumé at a glance. If the pages should become separated, he will know how many he should have.

(5) Use underlinings and dividing lines to help the prospective employer refer to specific material at a glance. Also follow the samples for the setting of margins.

(6) After you have entered the type of work desired, explain your experience and past performance of this work in detail. Omit any reference to occupational levels, such as "manager" or "assistant to the president," until the time of the personal interview. If the prospective employer has no upper managerial positions at the time, he may discard your résumé. If, however, you leave yourself open for possible positions at any managerial level, he could have something else for you.

(7) Choose carefully the general areas of experience to be placed in the wide margin of your résumé. The specific positions you have held in this area are then detailed in reverse chronological order. This is the accepted setup, but you can also place experience that bears most directly on your field at the top, regardless of chronological order.

(8) Normally, you do not furnish a photograph of yourself. In some states, the law forbids employers to

request a picture. However, if you wish, it is best to furnish a good passport-type photo to the employer.

(9) When you have completed your résumé, check it carefully against the samples, and then recheck your own information. If your résumé deviates from the form of the sample, be certain that you have good, strong reasons for that deviation.

What to Avoid in Preparing Your Résumé

(1) Never send carbon copies of your résumé to an employer.

(2) Never use abbreviations, especially the term "etc." Anything important enough to be stated should be written out.

(3) Do not go into much detail about work below your top level of employment.

(4) Some authorities suggest you find out about the company's level of salary before your interview. Save discussion of salary for the personal interview. A high salary asked on your résumé may harm your chances of getting an interview at all; bear in mind that high-paying jobs are not too plentiful.

(5) Do not limit yourself to area, salary or position desired without considering which of these is most important to you, or if any are more important than a chance for advancement. Be sure you know which of these you would be most willing to sacrifice.

(6) Know beforehand whether you will accept a step-down in authority and responsibility. Do not expect to start at or near the top. In business, time is needed to prove your ability unless you belong in the executive echelon. You cannot start at the top, no matter how good you are, or think you are. Remember that a

business firm will pay you only for what you can contribute.

Comparison of the Four Most Favored Résumés

As mentioned earlier, the four most favored résumés in use today are the *basic*, the *chronological*, the *functional* and the *modern analytical* résumés.

The following pages present a sample of each type of résumé for a mechanical engineer. The profession is a random choice. The samples could apply to, or be adapted for, any other profession.

A Mechanical Engineer in a Basic Résumé

RÉSUMÉ OF

Donald L. Campbell
151 E. 90th Street
New York, NY 10028
Date:
Phone: (212)838-9671

PERSONAL DATA

Born: 9/10/19 . . .
Married, 3 children
Excellent health
Height: 5' 11"
Weight: 175 lbs.
Willing to relocate
within U.S.A.

OBJECTIVE

Want to secure a position as Mechanical Engineer, where extensive background and experience are needed, and where a future is offered.

As an experienced Mechanical Engineer, worked mostly on the design and manufacture of motors and machines for producing, transmitting and using power. Designed and developed machines and parts that generate power, such as internal combustion engine, and machines that use power, such as heating, refrigeration and air conditioning units, lathes, machine tools, fans and presses.

WORK RECORD

19 . . . to Present
Aluminum Company of America, Inc., New York, NY
Senior Mechanical Engineer

19 . . . to 19 . . .
National Heater Co., St. Paul, MN
Mechanical Engineer

19 . . . to 19 . . .
Carrier Corp., Syracuse, NY
Mechanical-Design Engineer

EDUCATIONAL BACKGROUND
B.M.E. (Bachelor of Mechanical Engineering), Rensselaer-Polytechnic Institute, Troy, NY

PERSONAL ACCOMPLISHMENTS
Patented device: Hot-Air Heating and Air Conditioning
Licensed as Mechanical Engineer in New York and Minnesota

MEMBERSHIPS
American Society of Mechanical Engineers, New York, NY
National Society of Professional Engineers, Washington, DC

SALARY
Expect opening salary in the $30,000s, subject to negotiation, plus fringe benefits.

REFERENCES
Gilbert Smith
240 Park Ave., New York, NY 10017

George L. Tonklin
318 Stickley Blvd., St. Paul, MN 55110

Edward Marsh
1173 Roosevelt Ave., Syracuse, NY 13210

A Mechanical Engineer
in a Chronological Résumé

RÉSUMÉ OF

Donald L. Campbell
151 E. 90th Street
New York, NY 10028
Date:
Phone: (212)838-9671

PERSONAL DATA

Born: 9/10/19...
Married, 3 children
Health: Excellent
Height: 5' 11"
Weight: 175 lbs.
Willing to relocate
within U.S.A.

OBJECTIVE

Looking for employment as an experienced Mechanical Engineer, where excellent background in Mechanical Engineering offers possibilities for promotion and financial advancement.

WORK RECORD

Senior Mechanical Engineer, 19... to present, Aluminum Company of America, 240 Park Ave., New York, NY 10017. Supervised eight mechanical engineers and supporting technicians. Largely responsible for design of new equipment.

Mechanical Engineer, 19... to 19..., National Heater Co., 318 Stickley Blvd., St. Paul, MN 55110. Took active part in the design of new products. Production followed own designs or designs supplied to the company by other authorities.

Design Engineer, 19 . . . to 19 . . ., Carrier Corp., 1173
   Roosevelt Ave., Syracuse, NY 13210. As design
   engineer and then job captain, prepared air-
   conditioning and heating designs for modern
   equipment. This company is primarily a manufacturer's sales organization.

EDUCATION
   B.M.E. (Bachelor of Mechanical Engineering),
   Rensselaer-Polytechnic Institute, Troy, NY

PERSONAL ACCOMPLISHMENTS
   Patented device: Hot-Air Heating and Air Condition-
      ing
   Licensed as Mechanical Engineer in New York and
      Minnesota

MEMBERSHIPS
   American Society of Mechanical Engineers, New York,
      NY
   National Society of Professional Engineers, Washing-
      ton, DC

SALARY
   In the $30,000s. Open to negotiation. (History of
   salaries available.)

REFERENCES
   Gilbert Smith
   240 Park Ave., New York, NY 10017

   George L. Tonklin
   318 Stickley Blvd., St. Paul, MN 55110

   Edward Marsh
   1173 Roosevelt Ave., Syracuse, NY 13210

A Mechanical Engineer
in a Functional Résumé

RÉSUMÉ OF

Donald L. Campbell
151 E. 90th Street
New York, NY 10028
Date:
Phone: (212)838-9671

OBJECTIVE

To be connected with a firm where the services of Mechanical Engineer with experience and background can be used and where there are possibilities for advancement.

SUMMARY OF FUNCTIONAL EXPERIENCE

Excellent experience and background as a Mechanical Engineer who can very easily take over as Chief Engineer; who can undertake industrial mechanical design; who possesses creative, imaginative qualifications for any mechanical and technological project; and who can motivate fellow workers to perform.

SUPERVISION AND MOTIVATION

Have had extensive experience in supervising and motivating engineers and technicians in the production process, from start to finish.

INDUSTRIAL MECHANICAL DESIGN

Possess experience in designing chemical plants, instrumentation and electronic devices, industrial and commercial air conditioning, ventilating and heating equipment. Can prepare drawings and calculations for plant equipment and operation.

CREATIVE AND IMAGINATIVE

Have conceived and carried out ideas for designing a convector radiator that met the requirements of professionals such as architects and other interior designers. My design helped my employer to assume the lead in the manufacture of special convector radiators. Developed several inventions: U.S. patent granted on one, patent pending on another.

MECHANICAL AND TECHNICAL FLEXIBILITY

Functioned as production engineer in designing and construction of petroleum oil blending and distribution plants, including instrumentation. Supervised the mechanical phases of my employer's and clients' plant projects. Am the kind of mechanical engineer who is concerned with the production, transmission and use of power.

WORK RECORD

19 . . . to Present
Senior Mechanical Engineer, Aluminum Company of America, Inc., 240 Park Ave., New York, NY 10017

19 . . . to 19 . . .
Mechanical Engineer, National Heater Co., 318 Stickley Blvd., St. Paul, MN 55110

19 . . . to 19 . . .
Design Engineer, Carrier Corp., 1173 Roosevelt Ave., Syracuse, NY 13210

EDUCATION

Mechanical Engineering Degree, Rensselaer-Polytechnic Institute, Troy, NY

PROFESSIONAL ACCOMPLISHMENTS

Patented device: Hot-Air Heating and Air Conditioning

48

Licensed as Mechanical Engineer in New York and
   Minnesota

PROFESSIONAL AFFILIATIONS
   American Society of Mechanical Engineers, New York,
      NY
   National Society of Professional Engineers, Washing-
      ton, DC

PERSONAL DATA
   Born: 9/10/19...,
      Glens Falls, NY
   Married, 3 children
   Health: Excellent
   Height: 5'11"
   Weight: 175 lbs.
   Willing to relocate
      within United States

SALARY
   In the $30,000s plus fringe benefits. (History of
   salaries available.)

REFERENCES
   Available on request.

_____

A Mechanical Engineer in a Modern Analytical Résumé

RÉSUMÉ OF
Donald L. Campbell
151 E. 90th Street
New York, NY 10028
Date:
Telephone:
(212)838-9671

SUMMARY OF EXPERIENCE

Ten years of experience in mechanical design and production, for producing more goods at higher quality and lower cost. Able to design tools, engines, machines and other equipment. Prepared specifications governing manufacturing, testing, assembly and delivery of mechanical equipment. Evaluated performance test data. Prepared summary reports and staff studies on research and design projects.

OCCUPATIONAL OBJECTIVE

To be associated with a firm where creative imagination in the mechanical field can be applied for mutual benefit. I have the ability to visualize new products to be added to a line, to estimate their costs and their return to the company, then to put them into design and finally into production.

HIGHLIGHTS OF EXPERIENCE
19 . . . to Present
Aluminum Company of America, Ltd.
New York, NY
Senior Mechanical Engineer. Responsibilities include

mechanical engineering in Chemical Department; supervise eight mechanical engineers and supporting technicians. Responsible for design and development of mechanical phases of clients' chemical-plant projects, instrumentation and electronic devices, industrial and commercial air conditioning, ventilating, heating equipment and facilities. Handle all activities from flow sheet, sizing of pipes, piping layout, layout and design, to calculation drawings for required plant equipment and operation.

19 . . . to 19 . . .
National Heater Company
St. Paul, MN
Mechanical Engineer. Designed convector radiator to meet specifications and requirements of architects for curtain walls and other building designs. Designed electrical unit heaters, central air-conditioning units and controls.

As a result of these designs, company became leading manufacturer of special convector radiators in the United States and Canada. Developed several inventions: U.S. patent granted on one, patent pending on another. Canadian patent granted on one.

19 . . . to 19 . . .
Carrier Corp.
Syracuse, NY
Design Engineer. Although primarily a manufacturing sales firm, Carrier also engaged in a very large design and construction business. As a design engineer and later as job captain, prepared air-conditioning and heating designs. Also performed project-engineer functions for the sale of equipment

51

to mechanical contractors. After retraining and relocation, performed functions of service manager and technical advisor for the service of large-tonnage Centrifugal and Absorption Chillers.

Position required imaginative designing in wide range of products and equipment. Functioned as operations engineer in designing and construction of petroleum oil blending and distribution plants, including instrumentation.

EDUCATION

Rensselaer Polytechnic Institute, Troy, NY
Bachelor of Mechanical Engineering Degree, 19 . . . Curriculum designed to allow as many electives as possible after completion of required mechanical-engineering courses. Design and manufacturing courses: engineering drawing, manufacturing processes, metallurgy, strength of materials, machine design, industrial engineering, manufacturing engineering. Power generation courses: chemistry, physics, dynamics of fluids, heat engineering, electrical engineering, combustion, heat transfer, thermodynamics.

EARLY BACKGROUND

Grew up in Glens Falls, NY. Father city treasurer of Glens Falls. Educated in the public schools in Glens Falls. Prepared for college at, and graduated from, Albany High School, Albany, NY. Played intramural football. Member of the basketball team. Member of glee club.

MILITARY SERVICE

U.S. Army, 19 . . .–19 . . ., attained rate of Master Sergeant.

PERSONAL INTERESTS

Interested in creating new mechanical devices. Enjoy swimming and tennis as time permits.

PROFESSIONAL AFFILIATIONS

American Society of Mechanical Engineers, New York, NY

LICENSES

Professional Engineer in New York and Minnesota

PATENTS

Device: Hot-Air Heating and Air Conditioning. Currently in production.

PERSONAL DATA

Born: 9-10-19..., Glens
Falls, NY
Married, 3 children
Health excellent
Height: 5' 11"
Weight: 175 lbs.
Willing to relocate
within United States.

SALARY

In the $30,000s. Open to negotiation. (History of salaries available.)

REFERENCES

Excellent references on request.

PART 2

The Four Types
of Résumés

5

Preparation of the
Basic Résumé

How to Prepare a Basic Résumé

If, in your search for a job, you think you do not
need a résumé, it is still helpful to follow certain
procedures. One of these is the preparation of a *basic
résumé*.

This type of résumé is a very effective outgrowth
of the letter of application that was in common use
until very recently, and that it was customary to present
in person when calling on manufacturing plants, workshops, construction projects, mechanical establishments and similar organizations. It is very well suited
to a semiskilled worker who is looking for a job locally
or who wishes to relocate elsewhere. The basic résumé
is also well suited to those who enjoy physical exertion,
like to follow instructions, enjoy the outdoors, possess
manual and finger dexterity and are mechanically
inclined.

This is a simple type of résumé, elementary in its
presentation. It has proved helpful not only to those

57

who think they don't need a résumé, but also to blue-collar workers and skilled manual craftsmen.

In this résumé you record any past work experience you have had, including part-time or summer work. You also note in this résumé the work you have done as a trainee, or under an on-the-job program, or as a regular employee, as well as the details of the formal education you have had, together with the applicable dates. To these facts you can add any skills you have developed in volunteer work you may have engaged in, or in the pursuit of leisure-time activities. Such avocational pursuits or hobbies can sometimes be the means of acquiring valuable skills and experience.

The basic résumé can be said to resemble a letter of application. It is prepared in the form of a letter, or what is known as a curriculum *vitae*.

Before you apply for a particular job, learn something about the firm and its products or the services it offers. Possessing this information will give you confidence and will also, during the interview, impress the interviewer.

When you are about to start for your interview, make a list of the names, addresses and telephone numbers of former employers, and of persons who will provide references as to your qualifications and character. On this list also outline your personal traits, such as being quick to anger or being impatient about taking orders from others. Doing this will help you acquire self-discipline and give you a feeling of self-assurance during a job interview.

If you have any disability, it is a good idea to mention it, because a job offered you might entail activities for which you are not fit physically. It is best to be honest about this to avoid embarrassment later. Or you may be willing to accept a position that other applicants refuse. For example, a job might call for late-evening hours or for working some weekends, or it might be in a neighborhood that is regarded as undesirable. If you are willing to overlook such undesirable aspects the employer might be favorably inclined toward you.

As we have already said, the basic résumé can be regarded as a *curriculum vitae*, or a very descriptive letter, especially suited to an unskilled or semiskilled person. It presents information on paper that usually (before the basic résumé was devised) was presented verbally. It is really a modern development of the old verbal form, over which it is a decided improvement, since it presents all information about the applicant in a graphic, well-organized manner.

Dividing your personal information under the following headings will make a very interesting basic résumé:

(1) Name and address.
(2) Kind of position wanted.
(3) Personal data: date of birth, condition of health, height, weight, marital status, number of children if any, willingness to relocate, etc.
(4) Work experience: what kind of work you have done up to the present, and what relation it has to the job you want.
(5) Training: what kind of schooling you have had. Did you learn your trade by means of an on-the-job program, or did you learn it through serving an apprenticeship?
(6) Of what organizations, societies or unions are you a member?
(7) State if your salary is open to negotiation or, if you are a union man or woman, whether it is in accord with union requirements. Also, if you are willing to relocate, you might bring up the

matter of whether the salary of the job you are seeking is in line with your earnings in your previous job, particularly as regards the current cost of living.

Occupational Inventory for a Basic Résumé

NAME AND ADDRESS

PERSONAL DATA
This entry should include information on the following, or on the entries that you consider more important:

Age
Citizenship
Number of children
Height
Weight
Physical limitations (if any)
Birth place
Single or married (optional)
State of health

WORK RECORD
List your former positions and give as much information as possible about each job, and length of experience in each field that interests you. Put all information in writing; later, you can extract pertinent sections for the résumé you are preparing.

EMPLOYMENT YOU ARE TRYING TO SECURE
The kind of work you are willing to accept and for which you consider yourself better qualified.

WILLING TO RELOCATE

Somewhere in the résumé you should mention whether you are willing or not willing to relocate.

SALARY

Specify if the salary is open to negotiation, or the minimum salary that is acceptable, or whether you will take what the employer offers.

REFERENCES

Write down the names and addresses of persons or companies that will give you a reference. Use your judgment as to their importance or recency.

SERVICE

If you have any military background and there is a possibility of matching the work done in the armed forces to the job you are seeking, it can be helpful to mention it.

Portfolio of Samples of the Basic Résumé

Automobile Mechanic—Basic Résumé

RÉSUMÉ OF
Donald H. Harper
498 Manor Lane
Pelham, NY 10803
Date:
Phone: (914)768-2945

PERSONAL DATA
Born: 3/6/19...
Good health
Last physical
6/10/19...
5' 10"
170 lbs.

OBJECTIVE
I am looking for new employment as an automobile
mechanic because my present employer is going out of
business, and also because new construction is being
considered on the site of the present garage and one of
the owners is retiring.

WORK EXPERIENCE & RECORD
Under supervision, I worked as automobile
mechanic's helper, made minor automobile repairs
and adjustments and replaced worn or broken parts.
Assisted more experienced personnel who specialized
in alignment and steering; worked on certain types of
automatic transmissions, tearing down motors and
cleaning and separating parts.

At present, I do repair work in addition to servicing automobiles: inspecting and testing to determine cause of faulty operation; repairing or replacing defective parts to restore vehicle to proper operating condition; and supervising such routine jobs as tuning engines, replacing piston rings, aligning front wheels and adjusting or relining brakes.

SERVICE IN THE ARMY

Maintained and repaired construction, earth-moving and support-type engineering equipment of portable crawler, skid and wheel-mount types, including power bridging equipment.

EDUCATION

High school graduate from Fordham High School, Bronx, NY. Besides the experience gained in the Army, I learned the trade of mechanic's helper in a garage. Gained thorough knowledge of automotive mechanical problems.

SALARY

Open to negotiation.

REFERENCES

Robert Cipriani, 2 Wilcox Ave., Yonkers, NY 10705
Charles J. Dewey, 341 Maspeth Ave., Flushing, NY 11378
Paul Solbert, 724 Roosevelt, Pelham, NY 10803

Carpenter (Building)—Basic Résumé

RÉSUMÉ OF
Dunklin S. Burton
178 Tulane Avenue
Little Rock, AR 72204
Date:
Tel: (501)456-7832

PERSONAL DATA
Born: 6/15/19 . . . in
Little Rock, AR
Married, three children
Health: good; no
physical limitations
Height: 6'0"
Weight: 195 lbs.

OBJECTIVE
Since I am a fully qualified carpenter, I am looking for permanent employment in installing millwork and in finishing hardware trimming. I can lay and finish hardwood floors, build stairs or siding, trim wallboards, doors, windows and hardware. I am a good cabinetmaker, but in general I want to do what is called "finishing" in the carpentry trade.

HIGHLIGHTS OF EXPERIENCE
American Construction Corp., 19 . . .–19 . . . Some of the major duties in this job were to install millwork and finish hardware, lay and finish hardwood floors, build stairs. In cooperation with other

carpenters, I was required to assemble structural elements and build structures that were neat and uniform in appearance. I left the job because the firm went bankrupt through poor investments and overexpansion on new construction.

Construction and Remodeling in Teaneck, NJ, 19...–19... Most of my work was in what is called "rough carpentry," that is, building and erecting wooden frames, installing interior and exterior trim, building concrete forms, pouring shutes, erecting wooden scaffolds and similar heavy carpentry work. Left because the doctor advised me to do "finish" carpentry that was less strenuous and to which, through my cabinet work, I am more inclined.

TRAINING BACKGROUND

At the insistence of my mother, I finished high school during the summers and worked weekends as a carpenter's helper. After I finished high school, took part in a four-year apprenticeship program as the best way to learn carpentry.

MEMBERSHIPS

Member of Local 116 of United Brotherhood of Carpenters and Joiners of America.

SALARY

I now get regular union wages, after going through the usual process of raises from apprenticeship rates until I reached the journeyman carpenter's rate.

REFERENCES

Mr. Robert J. Villa, Bechtel Corp., San Francisco, CA 94102

Mr. Jimmi Jones, Ramada Development Corp.,
  Phoenix AZ 85012
Mr. Ed. W. Darien of Graziona Construction Co.,
  Pittsburgh, PA 15205

Construction Operating Engineer—
Basic Résumé

RÉSUMÉ OF
   Norman J. Gerrard
   175 Ohio Boulevard
   Cleveland, OH 73556
   Date:
   Phone: (216)789-5674

PERSONAL DATA
   Born: Cleveland,
      3/27/19...
   Married, no children
   Weight: 180 lbs.
   Height: 5'10"
   Willing to relocate; wife
      is stenographer and
      typist

OBJECTIVE
   I am an experienced engineer, skilled in construction-machinery operations, and am looking for steady employment with a large construction company. Can relocate to different projects in different parts of the country, or in foreign countries. I am skilled in the operation of several different and complex construction machines. Am also experienced in the manipulation of such machines as cranes, bulldozers, derricks, etc.

WORK RECORD
   Worked with Rusch Engineering Corp., Dallas, TX, operating earthboring machine. Was highly trusted

for my ability to set proper auger (drill) in spindle, start machine and stop boring at correct depth. For a time I was identified on some construction projects according to the names of the different machines.

On offer of a better salary, accepted a position with McKee Construction Co., Cleveland, OH, where I operated and controlled bulldozers, cranes, trench excavators and other types of construction machinery, including those that were more complex. These contractors undertook diversified projects, including highways, dams, airports and others of a large-scale type.

Before I became a journeyman operating engineer, I completed the regular three-year apprenticeship course. When required, I can undertake repair of equipment.

MEMBERSHIPS

International Union of Operating Engineers, Washington, DC
Associated General Contractors of America, Inc., Washington DC

SALARY

Expect the hourly rate for those who can operate cranes, bulldozers, air compressors. Open to negotiation, however, in accordance with the cost of living and location of job.

REFERENCES

Mark Robbinson, Rush Engineering Corp., Dallas, TX 75209
William G. Rogers, McKee Construction Co., Cleveland, OH 44135

G. J. Loppen, Loppen Construction Equipment Co.,
Chicago, IL 60612
Bill N. Kaplan, Chicago Leasing Construction Equipment, Chicago, IL 60606

Power-Truck Operator—Basic Résumé

RÉSUMÉ OF
Mike L. Klein
8001 Carlin
Detroit, MI 48228
Date:
Phone: (313)585-1202

PERSONAL DATA
Born: 6/7/19...
Married
Height: 5'10"
Weight: 159 lbs.
Excellent health
Willing to relocate

OBJECTIVE
Would like to connect with a company that needs the services of a reliable power-truck operator who has stamina and is responsible. The salary has to meet the requirements of the union or the cost-of-living index in the section of the country where the job is located.

WORK EXPERIENCE AND RECORD
Loading and Moving Materials Operator. MWA Company, Owosso, MI, 19... to 19... As the truck operator, my duties included loading and removing materials from stock located in different warehouses.

Power-Truck Operator. Magline, Inc., Pinconning, MI, 19... to 19... In this job my chief responsibility was seeing to it that all the power trucks were kept in good condition by cleaning, oiling, checking the water in the batteries and making simple adjustments as needed.

Power-Truck Operator. Meyers Industries, Inc., Tecumseh, MI, 19... to 19... As operator of a power truck that was equipped with lifts, I had to be careful to see how much the truck could lift and how much merchandise it could carry.

TRAINING

Learned to operate the power truck through on-the-job training. Had to pass very strenuous physical; received high rating in manual dexterity and mechanical ability, have above-average eyesight, including good depth perception.

REFERENCES

Mr. Ralph Rooney, MWA Company, Owosso, MI 48867

Ms. Margaret McTamney, Magline, Inc., Pinconning, MI 48650

Mr. Stanley Green, Meyers Industries, Inc., Tecumseh, MI 49286

RÉSUMÉ OF
William H. Hill
20 Court Street
Brooklyn, NY 11222
Date:
Tel: (212)657-8977

PERSONAL DATA
Born: 6-7-19 . . .
Weight: 160 lbs.
Height: 5' 9"
Excellent health

OBJECTIVE
Because of my experience and skill in sheet-metal work, I wish to transfer from the construction field to the manufacturing industry. I know how to avoid waste through proper calculations and through my ability to read blueprints and drawings made by the architect.

WORK EXPERIENCE
I have experience in installing ducts for ventilating, air-conditioning and heating systems in different locations. My most important experience has been through learning the complete routine of determining the size and type of metal needed before cutting with hand snips, power-driven shears and other tools, depending on the size of the job. Most of the work was done in industrial and commercial buildings. I acquired all this experience with a company that employed me for four years.

After becoming a member of the Sheet-Metal Workers' International Association, I got a job with Harris Bros., sheet-metal contractors, in Englewood, New Jersey. I was getting along fine in my new position, but after eighteen months, I had to resign because of my wife's health, due to a bronchial infection, required that I move to a different location.

TRAINING

I am a high school graduate. After graduation, I began to work with the sheet-metal Services Corp. under their on-the-job training program.

SALARY

The salary that is acceptable is the hourly requirement of my Union.

REFERENCES

John N. Meyers, Contractor, 140 So. Englewood Blvd., Englewood, NJ 07035 (201)476-1564

Ralph Markowitz, 27 Court St., Brooklyn, NY 11223 (212)765-7896

James L. Rollins, 340 Orange Rd., Montclair, NJ 07008 (201)498-7654

Benjamin Keller, 340 Fulton St., Brooklyn, NY 11020 (212)697-4831

Tool and Die Maker—Basic Résumé

RÉSUMÉ OF
Victor L. Boyd
645 Wilshire Blvd.
Los Angeles, CA 90017
Date:
Phone: (213)567-7834

PERSONAL DATA
Born: 7/16/19...
Married
2 Children
Height: 5' 8"
Weight: 185 lbs.
Willing to relocate
Own car

SUMMARY OF EXPERIENCE
A craftsman with ten years of experience working continuously in tool and die making. A tool and die maker is highly skilled and creative in the production of metal parts. He has to be experienced in the preparation of jigs and fixtures, and must also know how to make gauges and other measuring devices for manufacturing precision metal parts. Have constructed metal dies to shape metal in stamping and forging operations. Am very capable in repairing worn or damaged dies, gauges, jigs and fixtures, as well as in designing tools and dies.

OBJECTIVE
To secure a position as tool- and die-maker foreman with a concern that can use and appreciate my

experience and ability, which includes knowing how to design with precision. Salary open to negotiation.

WORK RECORD

> *Tool and Die Maker,* Air Transport Mfg. Corp., Los Angeles, CA 19 . . . to Present
>
> *Tool and Die Maker,* Everett/Charles, Inc., Pomona, CA 19 . . . to 19 . . .
>
> *Tool- and Die-Maker Assistant,* Concise Casting Corp., Hayward, CA 19 . . . to 19 . . .

TRAINING

> Attended high school. Most of the four years were spent in practical shop, training under a tool and die apprenticeship.

REFERENCES

> Mr. George T. Hamilton, 15 Weldon Ave., Los Angeles, CA 90065
>
> Mr. William A. Jackson, 300 Gramercy, Pomona, CA 91767
>
> Theodore S. Roosevelt, 201 Havana Ave., Hayward, CA 94544

Welder—Basic Résumé

William J. Rogers
813 La Paz Lane
Riverside, CA 92501
Date:
Phone: (714)754-9876

PERSONAL DATA
Born: 7/8/19 . . .
Married
Good health
Height: 5' 11"
Weight: 190 lbs.
Will relocate
Own car

OBJECTIVE
Looking for employment with a company that can use a skilled welder who can plan and lay out work from blueprints or other specifications. Capable of holding the position of welding foreman. Possess manual dexterity, good eyesight and good eye—hand coordination.

WORK EXPERIENCE & RECORD
It took several years under on-the-job training as a helper to become an experienced welder. Now I am a welder who can do arc or gas welding and am considered skilled in both. I also have experience in joining metal parts. I can do welding work on automobiles, spacecraft, airplanes, household appliances and many other products. I can do arc or

gas welding manually or by machine, and I am very familiar with the most modern welding equipment when done manually, having done this type of work for:

Angeles Welding & Mfg. Co., Inc., Santa Fe Springs, CA 90670, 19 . . . to 19 . . .

Certified Spotwelding Corp., Burbank, CA 91502, 19 . . . to 19 . . .

Wyle Laboratories, El Segundo, CA 90245, 19 . . . to 19 . . .

MEMBERSHIPS

Riverside Lions Club, Riverside, CA

The American Welding Society, Miami, FL

Member of Local 75 of the International Union, United Automobile, Aerospace and Agricultural Implements Workers of America, Riverside, CA

SALARY

Union wages of the community where I will be located.

REFERENCES

Mr. James Blake, Angeles Welding & Mfg. Co., Inc., Santa Fe Springs, CA 90670

Mrs. Elizabeth Peterson, Certified Spotwelding Corp., Burbank, CA 91502

Mr. Daniel Resnick, Wyle Laboratories, El Segundo, CA 90245

6

Preparation of the Chronological Résumé

How to Prepare a Chronological Résumé

The *chronological résumé* presents the information in somewhat more detailed form than does the basic résumé. It is favored by office workers, white-collar assistants, sales personnel and service employees. It is also useful for those in the skilled crafts and similar occupations, including semiskilled blue-collar workers. The occupational inventory for this type of résumé usually records experience in chronological order, following the details of education and job descriptions. If you have held many jobs, be careful not to waste valuable space by listing and describing work that is in no way related to the job you are now seeking.

The chronological résumé offers the best opportunity to present details of experience exactly as they occurred without any explanations. The information is arranged in *reverse* chronological order, showing the applicant's growth and development—characteristics that employers take special note of.

In that section of the résumé where you list previous jobs, you start with the last job and follow back in succession to your first job. The following is suggested as a possible arrangement for the chronological résumé:

(1) Name and address.
(2) Personal Data.
(3) Work record: Start each entry with the number of years you were on the job, the title of the position, if any, and the names and addresses of the companies. If you have any particular accomplishments that relate to the jobs held, then describe them as best you can to supplement the entry.
(4) Give the kind of training and experience you acquired, and above all try to emphasize the type of work you prefer.
(5) Refer to your memberships in the community and in the trade, and to whether you are a union man.
(6) Explain about the salary you expect in relation to the job, and state if you are willing to negotiate a new salary.
(7) List references.

The chronological résumé is justly favored because it is so easy to prepare. Nevertheless, some employers recognize its limitations with regard to special skills or special types of experience an applicant may have. Therefore, in using the chronological résumé, be sure to take special care in describing your jobs and your special skills.

Occupational Inventory for a
Chronological Résumé

NAME AND ADDRESS

Begin preparing your résumé by writing down your name, address and telephone number.

OCCUPATIONAL OBJECTIVE

The objective is a short description of your occupational goal. Include only the salient points of the position you desire.

WORK RECORD

List your former positions and give as much information as possible about each previous job and length of experience in the fields that you mention. Put all information you have in writing; later you can extract pertinent material for your résumé.

Do not fool yourself about your skills. You may be tempted to try, but you must be honest with yourself. Start by listing jobs that you can do well, such as auditor, bookkeeper, statistician. If you are a graduate of a business administration course, you are probably equipped to hold a position in an accounting department or in a statistical division. But you should not mention work just because it sounds interesting unless it is an activity that you want to explore and for which you have the proper educational background and personal aptitude.

EDUCATIONAL BACKGROUND

Under the entry Education, list all the training you have had, name all the institutions where you have studied and give the dates of attendance. This record must be clear, because many firms like to have a full chronological description of your education and dates of attendance at each institution. Show all courses taken, whether they are single subjects or part of a complete program of study.

SERVICE

If you have served in the armed forces of the United States, you should mention this fact, to show how you have spent your time in the past.

SALARY

Specify your salary range. On a separate piece of paper, list your salary history to submit on request. (But there are disadvantages as well as advantages to including this information; use your judgment.)

REFERENCES

Submit on request. (Collect letters of recommendation from past employers to have available when requested. Make duplicates so that you will not have to part with the originals.)

Portfolio of Samples of the Chronological Résumé

Accountant Assistant— Chronological Résumé

RÉSUMÉ OF
Constance J. Blackwell
377 Clark Avenue
Chicago, IL 60611
Date:
Tel: (312)697-4899

PERSONAL DATA
Born: 5-6-19 . . .
Single
Height: 5'4"
Weight: 118 lbs.

OBJECTIVE
To be associated with a large firm where my background, interests and mathematical aptitude can be applied for future development.

WORK RECORD
Accountant Assistant, Jones & Jones Corp., Chicago, IL, 19 . . . to 19 . . . Maintained general ledger that contained fund reports, records and files. Performed fiscal accounting by checking moneys committed or obligated.

Senior Bookkeeper, Alvado Transportation Co., Los Angeles, CA, 19 . . . to 19 . . . Verified disbursement documents for material and real property and for contractual services including utilities, communications, transportation of objects and other services. Kept accounts to reflect status of available funds.

EDUCATION

B.S. Degree in Business, Price College, San Diego, CA, June 19... Majored in accounting. Other courses included managerial statistics, business finance, marketing research, business mathematics and mathematics for computers. All college expenses paid by family allowance and part-time earnings.

MEMBERSHIP

Member of the National Association of Accountants, New York, NY
Illinois Accounting Society, Chicago, IL

SALARY

In the $15,000s plus complete fringes. Open to negotiation.

REFERENCES

William M. Feito, 1030 N. Dearborn, Chicago, IL 60611
Henry Lebowitz, 617 E. 23rd Street, New York, NY 10016
Emmanuel Klein, 210 Chicago Blvd., Evanston, IL 66003

Air-Conditioning and Refrigeration Technician—Chronological Résumé

RÉSUMÉ OF
   Edward E. Barnes
   3 Berrymeade Lane
   Dallas, TX 75234
   Date:
   Phone: (214)567-7634

PERSONAL DATA
   Born: 6/7/19 . . .
   Married
   No children
   Height: 6' 1"
   Weight: 175 lbs.
   Will relocate

OBJECTIVE
   Want a job with a company that needs someone experienced in air-conditioning, refrigeration and heat-distribution work in homes, offices, schools and other buildings, and that will afford opportunities for development and promotion.

WORK RECORD
   19 . . . to 19 . . .
   Air Conditioning and Refrigeration Technician. Alton Mfg. Co., Dallas, TX. When air-conditioning and refrigeration equipment broke down, I had to diagnose the cause and make the necessary repairs, while looking for defects. I inspected components, such as relays and thermostats. This company produces special kinds of window air-conditioners, and also small refrigerators, mostly for office use.

19 . . . to 19 . . .

Air-Conditioning and Refrigeration Mechanic. Command Air Corp., Waco, TX. Here I had to install and repair equipment ranging in size from small window units to large central air-conditioning or refrigeration centrals or refrigerators. When installing new equipment, it was my job to place motors, compressors, evaporators and other components in place, according to blueprints and design specifications.

19 . . . to 19 . . .

Mechanic Assistant. San Antonio Refrigerators, Inc., San Antonio, TX. As an assistant, helped the regular technicians to connect duct work, refrigerant lines and other piping, and then to connect these to an electrical power source. Helped in checking proper operation and functioning.

EDUCATIONAL BACKGROUND

Have a high school diploma from Johnson High School, Dallas, TX. Attended Dallas Technical Institute, where I earned a diploma as mechanical technician. Acquired a great deal of knowledge and skill as helper, beginning with simple jobs and progressing to jobs that were more complicated.

SALARY

Received regular salaries from the companies I worked for. The salaries were generally supplemented by opportunities for free-lance work during nonworking hours and weekends. History of regular salaries available on request.

REFERENCES

John Marsh, 28 Falls Dr., Dallas, TX 75211
Peter Wayne, 3 Santa Fe, Waco, TX 76710
Charles Burton, 100 Century Dr., San Antonio, TX 78242

Aircraft Mechanic—Chronological Résumé

RÉSUMÉ OF
Andrew L. Bellini
13 N. Rembrandt Circle
Pasadena, CA 92667
Date:
Phone: (213)766-1356

PERSONAL DATA
Born: 6/7/19...
Single
Good health
Height: 5' 9"
Weight: 152 lbs.
Will relocate to Florida or Texas

OBJECTIVE

To secure a job as an aircraft-maintenance supervisor,
where my background in aircraft maintenance and
coordinator of the work in the shops can be of importance to the company and to me financially.

WORK RECORD

19...–19...

Aircraft Mechanic. Intercontinental Airlines, Los
Angeles, CA. Most of my work in this job was
preventive maintenance. Changed engine oil,
greased wheel bearings, replaced spark plugs and
performed other minor tasks.

19...–19...

Aircraft Mechanic. West Coast Airlines, Pasadena, CA.
Most of my work on this job was on engines. Took

them apart, checked different parts for wear and replaced bearings or other parts as needed.

19...–19...

Assistant Aircraft Mechanic. Pan American Airways, Los Angeles, CA. Joined this company on leaving the Army. Performed all the work and acquired the experience that was necessary to obtain an airframe-mechanic license as well as a license for power-plant mechanic specializing in engines. Since then I have been very useful helping in F.A.A. inspections.

TRAINING

Graduate of Sera High School, Pasadena, CA, 19... Specialized in mechanics.

MILITARY SERVICE

After graduating from high school, joined the Army, where I trained as aircraft mechanic. Took a 21-week course for aircraft-maintenance supervisors (67Z). Learned how to supervise aircraft maintenance and coordinate work flow. Assigned work in the shop section and received instruction in proper work techniques and layouts for maintenance shops.

SALARY

In the $18,000s. Open to negotiation, according to benefits and duties. (History of salaries available.)

REFERENCES

David Hartman, 15 Ridgewood Lane, Pasadena, CA 91103

Rita Hill, 2400 East 26th Street, Los Angeles, CA 90058

Mike O'Connor, 101 Sheridan Ct., Riverside, CA 92504

Bank Teller—Chronological Résumé

RÉSUMÉ OF
Gloria L. Sainz
100 Clarendon Drive W
Dallas, TX 73208
Date:
Tel: (214)389-0191

OBJECTIVE
To secure a position as head teller or supervisor of specialized department. Possess experience in such banking duties as paying and receiving, savings, payroll, securities, notes teller and Christmas Club. Expect salary that is commensurate with the duties and responsibilities of the job. (History of previous salaries available.)

PERSONAL DATA
Born: 2/17/19 . . . in
San Antonio, TX
Married
Health: Good; no
physical handicaps
Height: 5' 6"
Weight: 130 lbs.
Residence: Own home;
willing to relocate if
the right opportunity
is offered
Hobbies: Tennis,
swimming; attend
ballgame when
possible

Affiliations: Garden Club;
Red Cross volunteer.;
worked in office
of General Hospital

WORK RECORD
   19 . . .–19 . . .
   Paying and Receiving Teller. Alamo National Bank, San
   Antonio, TX. Major duties were receiving deposits
   and paying out moneys withdrawn, after proper
   identification.

   19 . . .–19 . . .
   Savings and Christmas Club Teller. Allied Merchants
   Bank, Port Arthur, TX. Had to take care of the
   deposits for savings as well as accreditation; ac-
   cepted and recorded deposits made to Christmas
   Club savings accounts.

   19 . . .–19 . . .
   Securities and Notes Teller. Amarillo National Bank,
   Amarillo, TX. Handled certain transactions for clients
   who used the services of the bank in buying securities or bonds. Also handled notes and similar
   transactions for clients who made loans.

   19 . . .–19 . . .
   Payroll Teller. Austin National Bank, Austin, TX. Was in
   charge of helping several personnel departments of
   a number of business and professional organizations in the community, in connection with payroll
   checks of employees and of those who used the
   services of the bank.

EDUCATION
   Graduated from Sam Houston High School, San Antonio, TX. Took a commercial course in a private

commercial college, San Antonio, TX. After graduation the college got me the first job in a bank.

REFERENCES

Harry L. Johnson, Austin National Bank, Austin, TX
Bill Blanket, Alamo National Bank, San Antonio, TX
Joseph D. Meley, Allied Merchants Bank, Port Arthur, TX
John N. Glenn, 375 Third St., Dallas, TX
Mark B. Headley, 368 Lincoln St., Dallas, TX

Biochemical Technician—
Chronological Résumé

RÉSUMÉ OF
Leslie J. Engle
555 Woodland Drive
Cincinnati, OH 45245
Date:
Phone: (513)476-0817

PERSONAL DATA
Born: 6/20/19 . . .
Married, 3 children
Good health
Height: 5' 9"
Weight: 135 lbs.
Driver's license

OBJECTIVE
To be connected with an industrial laboratory of pharmaceutical company for analysis of urine, blood, spinal fluid and gastric juices for presence and quantity of metabolic substances, for by-products such as sugar, albumin and acetone bodies and for various chemicals, drugs and poisons.

WORK RECORD
19 . . .–19 . . .

Biochemical Technician, Melo Park Hospital, Cincinnati, OH. As a biochemical technician, assisted biochemists in analysis of biological substances, blood and other body fluids, foods and drugs. Most of the work involved conducting experiments and reporting their results to the supervising biochemist.

19...–19...

Biochemical Technician, Lindsay Laboratories, Inc., Stanford, CA. In this position have had to work primarily in the study of insects and insect control, and to help in developing new insecticides, and in determining how to use insects to control other insects or undesirable plants.

EDUCATION

B.S. Degree in Biochemical Science, June 19..., University of Cincinnati, Cincinnati, OH. Majored in the biochemical program offered for technicians, which included required arts courses. Among the courses taken were organic preparations, physical chemistry, food production, biology, bacteriology, qualitative organic analysis, and chemistry of nutrition. College expenses, financed through family allowance. On graduation, the Placement Service of the university secured me my first job with Melo Park Hospital.

MEMBERSHIPS

American Chemical Society, Washington, DC
American Institute of Biological Science (AIBS), Washington, DC

SALARY

In the $15,000s plus fringe benefits.

REFERENCES

George L. Bidwell, 3705 Walton Creek R., Cincinnati, OH 45227
Thomas J. Brown, Melo Park Hospital, Cincinnati, OH 45208
Frank Galleghar, Lindsay Laboratories, Stanford, CA 94305
James E. Hilton, 1450 W. Warner Ave., Chicago, IL 60613

Business-Machines Service Technician—Chronological Résumé

RÉSUMÉ OF
>   Edward Token
>   899 Boston Road
>   Cleveland, OH 44147
>   Date:
>   Phone: (216)786-5677

PERSONAL DATA
>   Born: 6/17/19 . . .
>   Married, 2 children
>   Good health
>   Height: 5' 9"
>   Weight: 170 lbs.
>   Willing to relocate

OBJECTIVE
>   19 . . . to present
>   To work as a service technician repairing and maintaining office equipment, such as the different kinds of typewriters and duplicating and copying machines.

WORK RECORD
>   19 . . . to 19 . . .
>   *Alkan Typewriters Corp.*, Cleveland, OH. Usually had to work in offices where the machines were used. The equipment was maintained under a monthly service fee, which required me to appear at least once a month to inspect, clean and oil the machines and to make minor adjustments. I often undertook selling the service, as I received extra commission for each customer I secured for the company.

Cleveland Typewriter Maintenance Service, Cleveland, OH. In this position I had to do the work in the shop on machines brought in by outside servicemen. The position offered considerable variety in working assignments. One of the most satisfying aspects of the job was that it gave me an opportunity to exercise my analytical ability in locating and correcting the cause of trouble in a malfunctioning machine.

TRAINING

After graduating from high school, I took a course in mechanics and obtained on-the-job training, work experience and instruction under the manufacturers' short explanatory courses offered by the makers of the different machines.

SALARY

Least accepted $200 weekly, plus all the required fringe benefits.

REFERENCES

Robert L. Wilson, 10 Blossom Ave., Cleveland, OH 44130

Milton Garrison, Cleveland Typewriter Maintenance Service, Cleveland, OH 44105

Steve L. Mills, 4800 W. 67th Street, Cleveland, OH 44144

Computer Service Technician—Chronological Résumé

RÉSUMÉ OF
> Robert G. Morrison
> 671 Continental Ave.
> Forest Hills, NY 11375
> Date:
> Phone: (212)345-2356

PERSONAL DATA
> Born: 7/9/19...
> Married, one daughter
> Health: excellent
> Last physical: 19...
> Height: 5' 9"
> Weight: 170 lbs.

OBJECTIVE

To work with a company that has a single installation, the size of which requires the services of a customer engineer full time. Can be of great help in programming, systems analysis, and servicing computer equipment.

WORK RECORD
> 19... to Present
> *Computer Customer Engineer*, Service Dept., Honeywell, Inc.
> New York, NY
> The duties in this position necessitate visits to customers to diagnose electronic failures. The position involves the use of certain specialized instruments designed for this type of work. After finding the

cause of the malfunction, repair can be undertaken. This job has required keeping up with technical information that is related to maintenance procedures and that computer manufacturers supply periodically.

19 . . . to 19 . . .
Assistant Field Engineer, Service Dept., Honeywell, Inc. New York, NY
In this job I worked under the direction of my supervisor in dealing with malfunctions by replacing faulty circuit boards, resoldering broken connections or repairing mechanical parts. Each job had to be finished as soon as possible to avoid loss of time and thereby save customer hundreds—possibly thousands—of dollars.

19 . . . to 19 . . .
Computer Service Technician,
Service Dept., Honeywell, Inc.
New York, NY
Here I served as helper in the installation of new equipment: laid down cables, hooked up electrical connections between machines, corrected any defects and tested the new equipment before the customer could use it. All work was done under the supervision of two computer customer engineers.

TRAINING
Graduated from Forest Hills High School, Queens, NY. Obtained an A.A. Associated Degree in Computing Service from the R.C.A. Mechanical Institute, New York, NY. At present working toward a degree as electrical engineer at Pratt Engineering School, Brooklyn, NY.

MEMBERSHIP

American Federation of Information Societies, Inc., Montvale, NJ

Institute of Electrical and Electronic Engineers, New York, NY

SALARY

Open to negotiation, according to hours and duties. (History of salaries available.)

REFERENCES

Excellent references on request.

Data-Processing Equipment
Operator—Chronological Résumé

RÉSUMÉ OF
Mayte P. Hamburger
854 West 180th Street
New York, NY 10033
Date:
Phone: (212)657-3545

PERSONAL DATA
Born: 7/12/19...
Single
Last physical: June
19...
Height: 5' 7"
Weight: 120 lbs.
Willing to relocate

SUMMARY OF EXPERIENCE
Operated any one or a combination of the following types of electrical accounting equipment: sorters, interpreters, tabulators, reproducers, card processors, collators, card punches, printers, tape duplicators, tape units on stored programs, optical scanners and other automatic data-processing equipment operated off-line from computer system.

WORK RECORD
19... to 19...
Digital-Computer Operator.
Data-Processing Information Service, New York, NY

19 . . . to 19 . . .
Digital-Computer Operator.
Multinumerical Advertising Services, Long Island City, NY

EDUCATION

A.A. Degree, Manhattan Community College, New York, NY, June 19 . . . Grew up in Jamaica, L.I., NY. Father worked with Grand-Penn Railroad. Attended public schools in Long Island; prepared for college in Jamaica High School, Jamaica, NY. Member of the Mathematics and English Clubs.

MEMBERSHIP

Data-Processing Management Association, Park Ridge, IL

SALARY

Salary in the $15,000s. (History of salaries available.)

REFERENCES

J. L. Angell, 680 Park Avenue, New York, NY 10016
John H. Aulick, 223 West 23rd Street, New York, NY 10011
Harold H. Epstein, 211 East 78th Street, New York, NY 10021

Electrocardiograph
Technician—Chronological Résumé

RÉSUMÉ OF
Louise H. Hilton
185 Cotton Tree Drive
St. Louis, MO 63141
Date:
Phone: (314)589-7654

PERSONAL DATA
Born: 3/7/19 . . .
Good health
Height: 5' 7"
Weight: 130 lbs.
Am not seeking
relocation

OBJECTIVE

To connect with a physician who is a cardiac specialist
and who, in addition to his general office practice, can
use an electrocardiograph technician. I wish to work
only during daytime hours.

WORK RECORD
19 . . . to 19 . . .
Electrocardiograph Technician and Physician's Assistant,
to Dr. Albert J. Heide, St. Louis, MO. He relocated his
practice to Dallas, TX.

19 . . . to 19 . . .
Electrocardiograph Technician, The Lutheran Hospital,
St. Louis, MO. In addition to my work in heart and
respiratory diseases, helped in attending the critical
patients.

19 . . . to 19 . . .

Electrocardiograph Technician, St. Lukes Hospital, St. Louis, MO. Worked as an assistant to the leading cardiac-services nurse, and had a fine opportunity to observe, and to practice my skill.

TRAINING

Graduated from Charles L. Lindbergh High School, St. Louis, MO. After graduating from high school, joined the Army, where I took a short, few-weeks course for specialist on electrocardiograph-basal metabolism rate (IN). Learned how to conduct tests to determine a patient's basal metabolism rate and how to take electrocardiograms in establishing the condition of the heart. Most of my training on the electrocardiograph was obtained through on-the-job work.

SALARY

Want a job as electrocardiograph technician with a private physician or hospital, where the remuneration is in line with standard salaries, and where I can work during the daytime hours.

REFERENCES

Dr. Albert J. Heide, 724 Cloverdale Lane, Dallas, TX 75234

Dr. William J. Brown, Cardiology Director of Lutheran Hospital, St. Louis, MO 73104

Ms. Agnes Feldmann, RN, Cardiology Div., St. Lukes Hospital, St. Louis, MO 73120

Dr. Henry L. Wilkson, Lutheran Hospital, St. Louis, MO 73104

Electroencephalographic
Technician—Chronological Résumé

RÉSUMÉ OF
   Elizabeth L. Boaz
   854 West 85th Street
   New York, NY 10033
   Date:
   Phone: (212)456-5322

PERSONAL DATA
   Age: ...
   Married, no children
   Good health
   Height: 5' 3"
   Weight: 120 lbs.
   Willing to relocate if the
      offer merits

SUMMARY OF EXPERIENCE
Have experience in the use, operation and maintenance of electroencephalographic apparatus for the diagnosis of brain diseases and infections. This electronic system records graphically the electrical activity of the brain. Neurologists and other professionals use EEG apparatus to help in diagnosing such disorders as epilepsy, tumors, the nature and extent of damage from injuries to the head and cerebral and vascular strokes.

In order to get results from the encephalograph that would be useful to the physician, I myself had to have some knowledge of medicine, anatomy and physiology. I used this knowledge in selecting the

correct machine settings so as to ensure certain levels
of consciousness and to be able to apply additional
electrodes for detecting abnormalities in the patient.

OBJECTIVE

To work in a hospital or medical center where electroencephalographic equipment is used, where there
is awareness of advances in this type of equipment
and where neurological disorders are among the chief
functions of the organization.

WORK RECORD

19 . . . to 19 . . .
Electroencephalographic Technician, Columbia-
Presbyterian Medical Center, Neurological Depart-
ment, New York, NY

19 . . . to 19 . . .
Electroencephalographic Technician, New York Hospital,
New York, NY

TRAINING AND BACKGROUND

Graduated from Clinton High School, New York, NY.
After graduation joined the Army, where I took a
12-week training course in the operation and maintenance of electroencephalographic apparatus, and in
how to help neurologists and neurosurgeons in their
work of detecting impaired areas of the human cortex.

MEMBERSHIPS

American Electroencephalographic Society
The American Medical Electroencephalographic Asso-
ciation
The American Society of Electroencephalographic
Technologists

REFERENCES

Dr. Mark B. Healey (Neurosurgeon), 1 Broad St., Philadelphia, PA 19107

Dr. Helen H. Nelson (Neurologist), Columbia-Presbyterian Medical Center, New York, NY 10032

Dr. William H. Beamis (Neurologist), New York Hospital, New York, NY 10021

Electrician (Construction)— Chronological Résumé

RÉSUMÉ OF
Mr. Philip T. Gobino
345 Washington
    Avenue
New York, NY 10033
Date:
Phone: (212)354-6687

PERSONAL DATA
Born: 19 . . .
Married
No children
Good health
Own car, and routine
    tools of the craft

OBJECTIVE
To be connected with a large construction company as a regular employee and not just through assignments on projects or through contracts executed by the company. I possess extensive background and knowledge in assembling, installing and performing as general electrician for the construction industry. I am familiar with problems relating to heat, light, power, air-conditioning and refrigeration, that operate through electrical systems.

WORK EXPERIENCE & RECORD
19 . . . to 19 . . .
Worked as a construction electrician on many different projects for *Santino Construction Co., Teaneck, NJ.* I was given the blueprints and specifications to be followed for different jobs. On the basis of these

blueprints and specifications I installed wiring and made decisions as to when I needed pipe and tubing inside partition walls or other concealed areas.

19 ... to 19 ...

Bareta Construction & Remodeling Co., New York, NY.
The work with this company consisted mostly of connecting wiring to circuit breakers, transformers or other components. The wires were joined by hand-soldering or mechanical means. When the job was finished, tested the circuits for proper connections and grounding.

TRAINING

After graduating from high school, was successful in being admitted to the apprenticeship program established by the International Brotherhood of Electrical Workers and the National Electrical Contractors Association. The apprenticeship lasted four years.

MEMBERSHIP

International Brotherhood of Electrical Workers, Washington, DC

SALARY

Salary according to the rates established by the union. Regular salary open to negotiation according to duties expected.

REFERENCES

Mario D. Valiente, Santino Construction Co., Teaneck, NJ 07666

Alfred Morrison, Bareta Construction & Remodeling, New York, NY 10022

Ralph H. Barriga, National Electrical Contractors Association, Washington, DC 20034

Electroplater—Chronological Résumé

RÉSUMÉ OF
Aaron L. Filippone
988 Washington Blvd.
Cleveland, OH 44110
Date:
Phone: (216)765-3456

PERSONAL DATA
Born: 3/7/19 . . .
Single
Height: 5' 7"
Weight: 155 lbs.
Willing to relocate

OBJECTIVE
To become part of the working force in a manufacturing company that uses electroplaters in production. Am an experienced electroplater and can also qualify as a supervisor or foreman of a department.

WORK RECORD
Electroplater Assistant, 19 . . . to present. C & R Products, Bedford, OH.
Have worked mostly in electroplating silverware and costume jewelry. The firm operates under contracts with manufacturers of different products that need electroplating.

Electroplater Inspector, 19 . . . to 19 . . . Mechanical Coatings, Inc., Cleveland, OH.
Had to inspect all plated parts to find any defects. Learned how to use certain specialized instruments for this type of work, such as micrometers, calipers and other devices.

Electroplater, 19 . . . to 19 . . . Chromium Corp. of America, Cleveland, OH.

As a helper, worked on a variety of small jobs, such as mixing solutions, plating, and watching the time needed on each project to get best possible finish.

TRAINING

Learned the work under an on-the-job program at Chromium Corp. Attended a vocational school where I took specialized courses in electroplating skills.

SALARY

Open to negotiation, but will not accept less than standard required by the union or by the responsibilities and duties of the job.

REFERENCES

Mr. Peter Finch, 38 Wingate Rd., Cleveland, OH 44137
Ms. Gladys Steward, 245 Ottawa Rd., Cleveland, OH 44105
Mr. Carl Snyder, 2000 East 35th St., Cleveland, OH 44115

Hotel Clerk—Chronological Résumé

RÉSUMÉ OF
Robert J. Brownell
500 Clark Ave.
San Antonio, TX 78210
Date:
Phone: (512)966-7234

OBJECTIVE

To secure a position as a hotel front-office clerk, with an opportunity to work with the public relations department and banquet manager in booking conventions and tourists. Seeking salary commensurate with duties and responsibilities of the job. (History of previous salaries available.)

PERSONAL DATA

Born: 3/16/19 . . . in
    Austin, TX
Married
Health: Good. No
    physical handicaps.
    Wear glasses.
Height: 5' 8"
Weight: 160 lbs.
Residence: Own home.
    Willing to relocate if
    right opportunity is
    offered.
Hobbies: Tennis,
    swimming, watching
    baseball
Affiliations: Rotary Club,
    YMCA

110

WORK RECORD

Desk Clerk. Alamo Hotel, San Antonio, TX, 19 . . . to present. Handle registrations and reservations. Advise housekeeper and telephone operators regarding incoming and departing guests.

Front-Office Clerk. Merchants Hotel, Port Arthur, TX, 19 . . .–19 . . . Accepted moneys and jewels to be kept in hotel safe. Registered guests. Issued keys and distributed mail.

Bellhop. National Hotel, Austin, TX, 19 . . .–19 . . . Took job after graduating from high school. Carried luggage for guests to their rooms. Opened the door. Described hotel facilities, dining-room hours, bar, cafeteria. Also provided information regarding special attractions available in city.

EDUCATION

Graduated from Sam Houston High School, Austin, TX

REFERENCES

Harry L. Johnson, National Hotel, Austin, TX
Ruben Blanket, Alamo Hotel, San Antonio, TX
Joseph D. Melbar, Merchants Hotel, Port Arthur, TX
Bill H. Glenow, 375 Third St., Dallas, TX
Mark B. Hadley, 368 Lincoln St., Dallas, TX

Instrumentation
Technician—Chronological Résumé

RÉSUMÉ OF
   John H. Buono
   310 East 36th St.
   New York, NY 10016
   Date:
   Phone: (212)685-9837

PERSONAL DATA
   Born: 6/8/19 . . .
   Married, one child
   Good health
   5' 10"
   170 lbs.
   Own car
   Personal finances in
      good order

OBJECTIVE
   To work for a firm where my experience and extensive
   knowledge of physical sciences as well as electrical-
   electronic and mechanical engineering can be
   utilized. Able to perform any one or a combination of
   the following tasks: install, repair, maintain and
   adjust recording, telemetering and controlling instruments. Disassemble malfunctioning instruments, and
   examine and test mechanisms and circuitry for defects.

WORK RECORD
   Instrumentation Technician. American Mechanical
      Corp., Brooklyn, NY, 19 . . . to present. Helped to

112

develop and design complete measuring control devices, such as those used in spacecraft, that sense and measure changes in heat or pressure, automatically record data and make necessary adjustments. Fabricate parts from metals, using watchmaker's lathe. Assemble and subassemble technical instruments.

Tool Designer. Tools and Mechanical Products, Inc., Long Island City, NY, 19 . . .–19 . . . My work was to design, or complete the final design from original sketches, of instruments needed for mass production. Often had to redesign existing tools to improve their efficiency. The engineer in charge usually made general pencil sketches for the design of such devices as cutting tools, jigs, dies, special fixtures and other attachments used in machine operations.

MILITARY SERVICE

United States Army, 19 . . .–19 . . . Technical Service Unit, Ft. Bliss, TX. Electronic-instrument repairman (38B)

EDUCATION

Graduated from Forest Hills High School, Queens, NY, 19 . . . Also attended the New York Technical Institute, New York, NY, 19 . . .–19 . . . Followed the program offered for technicians specializing in instrumentation. Took courses that gave me practical knowledge in maintaining and repairing instruments such as meters and similar devices.

SALARY

In the $18,000s plus complete fringe benefits. (History of salaries available.)

REFERENCES

John J. Veliz, 435 West 50th St., New York, NY 10019

Jerome Billings, 16 Court St., Brooklyn, NY 11212

James H. Blake, 130 West 47th St., New York, NY 10036

Martha A. Gonzalez, 177 West 181st St., New York, NY 10033

Insurance-Claim Adjuster—
Chronological Résumé

RÉSUMÉ OF
  Raymond D. Larsen
  854 West 180th Street
  New York, NY 10033
  Date:
  Phone: (212)768-9356

PERSONAL DATA
  Born: New York, NY;
    9/15/19 . . .
  Enjoy excellent health
  Height: 5' 10"
  Weight: 182 lbs.
  Willing to relocate for
    the proper opportunity

OBJECTIVE
  Looking for a job as insurance-claim adjuster-
  supervisor in New England territory. (History of
  salaries available on request.)

SUMMARY OF BACKGROUND
  Extensive experience as insurance-claim adjuster.
  Familiar with investigating, adjusting, negotiating
  and settling claims after policyholders suffer losses.
  Know how to sell property and liability insurance.
  Adjusted and made certain that settlements were in
  line with losses. Always investigated to protect my
  employers from false or inflated claims. Submitted my
  findings to insurance company that paid the claimant.

WORK RECORD

Insurance-Claim Adjuster (New York territory) American Home Assurance Co., New York, NY; 19... to present

Claim Adjuster-Investigator (Newark territory) Aetna Life Insurance Co., Hartford, CT; 19...–19...

Claim Adjuster-Settler (New York territory) American Progressive Health Insurance Co., New York, NY; 19...–19...

Claim Adjuster-Investigator (New York territory) Associated Madison Companies, Inc., New York, NY; 19...–19...

EDUCATION

High school graduate, Richmond Hill High School, New York, NY, 19...–19... Attended Lehman College, Bronx, NY, 19...–19..., majoring in accounting, business administration, merchandising psychology. Took specialized course in insurance to help me in the examination for the state license required for an insurance-claim adjuster. The on-the-job training I received was also very helpful when I took the exam.

MEMBERSHIPS

Member of the Republican Club, New York, NY
Member of Eastside Bowling Club, New York, NY
Member of the National Association of Public Adjusters, Baltimore, MD

REFERENCES

Harry Maverick, American Home Assurance Co., 20 Park Ave., New York, NY 10017
Joseph Jefferson, Aetna Life Insurance Co., 45 Bates Place, Hartford, CT 06114
Louis Daniels, Associated Madison Companies, 245 Madison Ave., New York, NY 10020

Marketing-Research
Assistant—Chronological Résumé

RÉSUMÉ OF
   Robert L. Taylor
   12 West Jackson Blvd.
   Oak Park, IL 60304
   Date:
   Phone: (312)457-8534

PERSONAL DATA
   Born: 8/9/19 . . . in
   Forest Park, IL
   Married—four children,
   aged 19, 14, 10, 9
   Health: Good
   Height: 6'0"
   Weight: 190 lbs.

OBJECTIVE
   Position in the Consumer Goods department or in the
   marketing and promotion of consumer goods.

WORK RECORD
   19 . . . to 19 . . .
   Morristown Marketing Service Corp., Chicago, IL.
   Marketing and research in the distribution and sales
   promotion of supermarket goods.

   19 . . . to 19 . . .
   Ajapan Distribution Corp., Evanston, IL. Research in
   obtaining new contractors in the distribution of
   radios, TVs, washing machines from wholesale
   warehouses.

117

19 . . . to 19 . . .

Plastics and Chemicals Corp., Skokie, IL. Director of marketing certain plastics and chemicals that serve as raw materials for housewares.

EDUCATION

B.A. in Business Administration, Northwestern University, Chicago, IL. Majored in marketing, research and transportation. Have successfully attended three workshops on marketing conducted by the Wharton School of Business in Philadelphia, PA.

MILITARY SERVICE

After basic training, was assigned to Army routine, purchasing general merchandise, especially consumer products. Remained in the services two years.

MEMBERSHIPS

American Marketing Society, Chicago, IL
Sales Executives Club of Chicago, Chicago, IL

CIVIC AFFILIATIONS

Head of company's annual Cancer Society meeting, Chicago, IL

SALARY

My salary is in the $25,000s—open to negotiation. (History of salaries available on request.)

REFERENCES

Available on request.

Nurse, Practical—Chronological Résumé

RÉSUMÉ OF
Margarite L. Feld
301 Lehmann Ct. North
Chicago, IL 60614
Date:
Phone: (312)678-9845

PERSONAL DATA
Born: 19 . . .
Marital status: single
Health: excellent
Height: 5'4"
Weight: 125 lbs.

SUMMARY OF EXPERIENCE
As a practical nurse I possess the necessary technical knowledge that enables me to provide nursing care under the direction of physicians and registered nurses. My duties consisted of the usual bedside care of patients, including the taking of temperature and blood pressure, changing clothes worn by patients, administering prescribed medicines and assisting patients in bathing and other personal aspects of hygiene.

PRESENT OBJECTIVE
To be connected with a private nursing home, where my practical knowledge and experience can be made available for the benefit and welfare of the patients and the credit of the institution. I am interested in a position in which the hours for work are under a straight shift and are not subject to constant change.

WORK RECORD

19 . . . to 19 . . .
Cook County Medical Center, Chicago, IL
Practical Nurse—Medical Therapy Division

19 . . . to 19 . . .
Chicago University Medical Center, Chicago, IL
Practical Nurse—Assisted in supervising the work in
the wards for patients.

19 . . . to 19 . . .
Highland Park Nursing Home, Highland Park, IL
Practical Nurse—In charge of attendance for six floors
occupied by patients. (This nursing home had to
close because of financial difficulties.)

EDUCATION

Took the regular course in practical nursing at Cook
County Medical Center, where I obtained my diploma.
Also passed the examination required for the license,
according to law.

MEMBERSHIPS

American Nurses Association, Kansas City, MO
National League of Nursing, New York, NY
National Federation of Licensed Practical Nurses, Inc.,
New York, NY

SALARY

Open to negotiation, on yearly basis, with corresponding fringe benefits. History of salaries available
on request.

REFERENCES

Margarite Klein, Director of Nurses, Chicago University Medical Center, Chicago, IL

Dr. Robert J. Feingold, Director of Physical Therapy,
Cook County Medical Center, Chicago, IL
Dr. Emil R. Howson, 1030 North Sheridan Rd.,
Chicago, IL

Patternmaker Technician—
Chronological Résumé

RÉSUMÉ OF
Jack M. Bassett
854 West 180th Street
New York, NY 10033
Date:
Phone: (212)876-9123

PERSONAL DATA
Born: 6/7/19 . . .
Height: 6'1"
Weight: 180 lbs.
Relocation only within the metropolitan area
Own car

OBJECTIVE
To secure a position within the metropolitan area of New York City that will use my craftsmanship and skill as a foundry patternmaker. Am experienced in using molds for metal castings, and can work with metal and wood, as well as plaster and plastics. Am accustomed to working from blueprints prepared by engineers. Know how to examine the pattern and detect any imprecisions for the intended product by carefully checking each dimension with such instruments as micrometers and calipers.

WORK EXPERIENCE AND RECORD
Material Sciences, Inc., New York, NY, 19 . . . to 19 . . .
Industrial Patternmaker Inspector. Supervised and inspected the work of more than 25 employees.

Utica Steam Engine & Boiler Works, Utica, NY, 19 . . . to 19 . . . Patternmaker. Prepared patterns from metal stock or from rough castings made from a wooden pattern.

Seals Easter, Inc., Red Bank, NJ, 19 . . . to 19 . . . Patternmaker Assistant. Helped in the casting and preparation of wood or plastic patterns, and learned the difficult basic principles of patternmaking.

TRAINING

High school graduate, Technical High School, New York, NY.

Attended the Mechanical Institute, New York, NY; took courses in metal designing and general mechanics.

SALARY

Need a salary in accordance with the cost of living in New York, and that is stipulated by the Union.

REFERENCES

Harry J. Friedman, 308 Park Ave., New York, NY 10016

Lawrence L. Timpson, 185 Java St., Brooklyn, NY 11222

Douglas Leigh, 724 Meadow Lane, Elizabeth, NJ 07201

Photoengraver—Chronological Résumé

RÉSUMÉ OF

    Colman B. Fountain
    1 Lakeview Avenue
    Bridgeport, CT 06606
    Date:
    Phone: (203)345-9652

PERSONAL DATA

    Born: 2/8/19 . . .
    Married, 2 children
    Height: 6'0"
    Weight: 165 lbs.
    Willing to relocate
    Own car

OBJECTIVE

Looking for employment with an engraving-manufacturing firm where my experience can be utilized for the benefit of the firm and for my own financial improvement.

WORK RECORD & EXPERIENCE

Bridgeport Engravers Supply Co., Bridgeport, CT, 19 . . . to 19 . . . Photoengraver Inspector. Worked as inspector and helper on the different steps of the engraving process. This company also sells supplies to photoengravers in the New England states.

Beck Engraving Company, Inc., Philadelphia, PA, 19 . . . to 19 . . . Photoengraver Assistant. Mostly, the work had to do with preparing the negatives and the proper plates for customers using the photo-offset process of printing.

Artcraft Engravers of Pittsburgh, Inc., Pittsburgh, PA, 19 . . . to 19 . . . Photoengraver Assistant. Started as helper and learned the skill through several years of on-the-job work. Also attended night school, supplementing the daily training.

MEMBERSHIPS

Graphic Arts International Union, Washington, DC
American Photo Platemakers Association, Chicago, IL
International Rotary Club

SALARY

Within the limits established by the union for the area where the job is located, the salary is open to negotiation.

REFERENCES

Max T. Oppenheimer, 35 Madison Ave., Bridgeport, CT 06604
Maurice C. Atkins, 601 E. Annsbury, Philadelphia, PA 19120
Elton Robinson, 6231 Penn Ave., Pittsburgh, PA 15206

Production Planner
Assistant—Chronological Résumé

RÉSUMÉ OF

Harry H. Long
15 Jackson Street
Little Falls, NJ 07424
Date:
Phone: (201)699-4777

PERSONAL DATA

Born: 5/2/19...
Excellent health
Height: 5'8"
Weight: 160 lbs.

OBJECTIVE

Completely satisfied with my present employment where there was every indication that I was going to be promoted to the post of supervisor. It happened, however, that my home and those of several others in the neighborhood burned to the ground. This is why I am looking for new employment with a better income.

WORK RECORD

19 . . . to 19 . . .

Sellis Manufacturing Company, Wayne, NJ. My job has been to coordinate the flow of work through the plant and report any trouble spots to the production engineer.

19 . . . to 19 . . .

Cooking & Houseware Equipment, Inc., Butler, NJ. The work in this job was mostly administrative. It involved the supervision and training of new workers.

126

I was also expected to help in the coordination of work among the different departments.

TRAINING

I am a high school graduate, Jefferson High School, Queens, NY. Took a one-year mechanical course at Steinmetz Vocational High School, Long Island City, NY.

SALARY

Open to negotiation related to the duties and requirements of the job.

REFERENCES

Robert H. Hill, Philadelphia, PA; (215)765-9723
William H. Harrison, Trenton, NJ; (609)295-5532
Paul L. Wigman, West Chester, PA; (215)789-4255
George B. Taylor, Reading, PA; (215)456-2891

Public-Relations Assistant— Chronological Résumé

RÉSUMÉ OF
Louise J. Hall
1 Main Street
Fort Lee, NJ 07024
Date:
Phone: (201)546-7892

PERSONAL DATA
Born: 19 . . .
Single
Excellent health
Height: 5'5"
Weight: 120 lbs.
Willing to relocate, if
   position merits

OBJECTIVE
A position in which my formal training in communications will be used, and where my potential can be realized.

WORK RECORD
Summer, 19 . . .
Time Magazine, New York, NY
Promoting new subscribers, Circulation Division

Summer, 19 . . .
Time Magazine, New York, NY
Assistant, Rewriting Division

Summer, 19 . . .
Hill & Knowlton, Inc., New York, NY
Assistant, News-Releases Dept.

Part-time employment
Hill & Knowlton, Inc., New York, NY
Evening and Christmas vacations during last year in
    college

EDUCATION
Columbia College, Columbia University, New York
    NY. B.S. in communications, 19 . . Scholastic hon-
    ors; on the Dean's List during the last three years of
    college.

Columbia University. Currently attending evenings,
    working toward a master's degree in public rela-
    tions.

INTERESTS
Writing, reading and ship-model building. Enjoy ten-
    nis, swimming, golf.

MEMBERSHIP
Public Relations Society of America.

SALARY
In the $15,000s—open to negotiation.

REFERENCES
On request.

Surveyor Assistant—
Chronological Résumé

RÉSUMÉ OF
   Garry Tompkins
   345 Pasteur Avenue
   Dallas, TX 75228
   Date:
   Phone: (214)389-1545

PERSONAL DATA
   Born: 3/18/19...
   Married, no children
   Health: good
   Height: 5'9".
   Weight: 170 lbs.
   Willing to relocate:
      national or
      international

SUMMARY OF EXPERIENCE
   My extensive experience includes the ability to determine the precise measurements and locations of elevations, points, lines and contours on the earth's surface, and the distances between points. When planning field work, I selected survey reference points and determined the precise location of natural and man-made features of the region surveyed. Also, when surveys were done by others, the results were usually turned over to me, to verify the accuracy of the survey data, the maps, sketches and reports. My immediate superiors appreciated my sense of responsibility in the performance of my duties.

OBJECTIVE
To be connected with a large construction company, or an oil company, that has continuous need for experienced surveyors.

WORK RECORD
19 . . . to 19 . . .
Topographic Surveyor. U.S. Geological Survey Bureau, Houston, TX

19 . . . to 19 . . .
Highway Surveyor. U.S. Forest Service, Waco, TX

19 . . . to 19 . . .
Land Surveyor. Bureau of Land Management, Houston, TX

TRAINING
Graduate, James Monroe High School, Oklahoma City, OK
A.A. in Surveying, Oklahoma Technical Institute, Oklahoma City, OK

LICENSES
Have land-surveyor licenses for Oklahoma, Texas and California.

SALARY
Open to negotiation, according to duties and location.

REFERENCES
Available on request from government agencies and from responsible private individuals.

Tabulating-Equipment
Operator—Chronological Résumé

RÉSUMÉ OF
Rose M. Kaplan
1602 Blackview Road
Chicago, IL 60615
Date:
Phone: (312)865-7634

PERSONAL DATA
Born: 9/6/19...
Good health
Height: 5'5"
Weight: 122 lbs.
Loop location preferred
Day shift only

OBJECTIVE
To secure a position where I can attend to machines that perform certain functions, such as sorting, interpreting, reproduction and collating. Batch system preferred to on-line system.

WORK RECORD
Media Communications Services, Inc.
Chicago, IL
19...–19... *Computer-Equipment Operator.* Operated on-line or off-line peripheral machines, transferring data from one to another print output, and read data into and out of digital computer. Operated electronic computer console and auxiliary equipment.

Computer Service Bureau, Inc.
Chicago, IL
19 . . .–19 . . . *Data-Processing Equipment Operator.* In this position I was able to apply my knowledge of several machines, such as 029 and 129, alpha and numeric machines, and I handled any one or a combination of the following: the controls of an electronic digital computer to process business, scientific, engineering or other data according to operation instructions; responsibility to correct computer errors or failures and to resume operations; and notification of supervisor of these or of work stoppages.

EDUCATION

Graduated from Jones Commercial High School, Chicago, IL. Among the courses I took were typing, mathematics, accounting and several on computer equipment.

Attended special course in programming at Wabash Commercial School, Chicago, IL, where I was also able to acquire a knowledge of the practical manipulation of several machines such as keypunch, verifier, cobol.

PERSONAL INTERESTS

Sewing, reading and swimming as time permits.

SALARY

In the $13,000s. Open to negotiation, if the opportunity merits.

REFERENCES

Louise Gray, 4148 N. Austin Ave., Chicago, IL 60634

Peter Mahoney, 2442 Marshfield Ave. S., Chicago, IL
  60608
Phillip Morgan, 1590 East 69th Place, Chicago, IL
  60637

Topographical Draftsman— Chronological Résumé

RÉSUMÉ OF

Phillip T. Bogino
4355 Memorial Dr.
Tulsa, OK 74115
Date:
Phone: (405)978-3456

PERSONAL DATA

Born: 7/9/19 . . .
Single
Height: 5'8"
Weight: 160 lbs.
Willing to relocate

SUMMARY OF EXPERIENCE

Am able to construct topographic-hydrographic maps, charts and mosaics from field survey data or aerial photographs, using drafting instruments. Applied knowledge of terrain representations and approved conventional map signs and symbols to plot planimetric and topographic details. Corrected and revised existing maps. Prepared grid drawings for mosaics and topographic maps.

OBJECTIVE

To work in the surveying department of an oil company where I can draw the proper maps; correct previous studies from source data, such as surveying notes, aerial photographs or other maps; and perform the duties in accordance with the requirements of the oil industry.

135

WORK RECORD

Central Oil Company, Topographic Division, Dallas, TX, 19...–19...

Oriental Oil Company, Topographic Drafter, Valencia, Venezuela, 19...–19...

Richmond Oil Company, Surveying Division, 19...–19...

EDUCATION

Graduated from Monroe High School, Phoenix, AZ, 19... Made good grades in all my courses, especially in drafting and mathematics (algebra, geometry and trigonometry).

MILITARY SERVICE

19...–19... After graduating from high school, joined the U.S. Army. Learned how to work with survey personnel and assist experienced surveyors. Took courses for cartographic draftsmen (81C) in the Army School—courses that covered a great deal of ground in the practice of topographic computing.

SALARY

In the $18,000s, according to location of position, duties assigned and possibilities for promotion. History of salaries on request.

REFERENCES

Mr. Roller J. Watson, 3 Glover Rd. NW., Washington, DC 20015

Mr. Gary L. Wilkins, 315 Devenwood Drive, Richmond, VA 23235

Mr. Ray Hoffman, 500 Nebraska Ave. N., Oklahoma City, OK 73117

Mr. Gilbert T. Brooks, 1677 Young Place E., Tulsa, OK 74106

7

Preparation of the Functional Résumé

How to Prepare a Functional Résumé

A *functional résumé* is organized according to the functions of a job. Some consider it the most basic and useful of the different kinds of résumés. When you analyze your work history for a functional résumé, you discover your own "hidden assets" and present them in such a way that they point directly to your next job. This type of résumé is especially suited to those who can express themselves effectively, who are interested in ideas, and who are inclined to creative or artistic activity.

Select only those facts from your total experience that relate to the job you are aiming for. Omit irrelevant items—if you have held many jobs, you may waste valuable space by including information that does not serve your purpose. Furthermore, you will probably include descriptions of work that are far below your present level of ability.

Concentrate on the kind of job you want and on the jobs you have held. For example, a technician might arrange the functional résumé according to the projects worked on, presenting each project in problem-and-solution form. A copywriter might base a functional résumé on the different kinds of copy written, or on the different media or products for which copy was written.

Organize your experience into a presentation of key qualifications for the job you want. Work with two lists: one relating to the functions of the job you seek, the other being your job-history worksheet. Beside each job description or accomplishment on the worksheet, write the corresponding function of your job goal.

Start by writing the title of the job you want on a separate piece of paper. List the key functions of the job in the left-hand margin, leaving plenty of space between them. If you have been comprehensive in your personal-inventory research, an employer will know that you understand what the job involves as he reads the captions. Immediately, he can determine whether or not you are qualified for the specific opening he has.

You will begin to discover that many functions of your future job were performed in various forms throughout your working experience. For example, you may have kept records on one job, or checked general entries on another, or worked as an assistant in the accounting department on a third. Experience in record-keeping can be very useful in accounting. In a functional résumé, this "hidden" accounting experience comes to light, and shows up more clearly than it would in a different form of résumé.

On the other hand, you may be just out of school, with your experience limited to part-time or summer work. A functional résumé may make you, a young trainee seeking a beginning job, appear as if you regard yourself a $25,000-a-year executive. If you have little experience in the field you seek, a letter of application compressing your qualifications into one or two paragraphs might be more effective. Stretched out in a functional résumé, the small amount of experience may appear trivial and sporadic. Personality, willingness to learn and evidence of potential ability are often more successfully projected in a good letter of application for a trainee position.

Though writing a functional résumé is not difficult, some men and women face certain problems with it. In giving themselves ample credit for their real capabilities, they often overreach themselves as regards salaries and job titles. Some are hesitant about making the connection between their self-appraisal and what is possible in the employment market. Bearing these small difficulties in mind, they can be readily overcome when using the functional résumé.

In preparing your functional résumé, the volunteer work you did and what you learned in other areas of living rate equal billing with paid employment. Thus, your stint as regional convention manager for a national organization would not, in the functional résumé, be buried under some routine heading such as "community activities." You can review and relate what you actually did in your volunteer role, from site surveys to bargaining, to staffing, to housing, to publicizing—right down to your final report. Depending on the job you are aiming at, you can play up the most relevant functions. For a department store, where women take charge of the fashion shows, you would emphasize your success in bringing disparate and sometimes temperamental groups together on schedule. Or if you proposed and undertook several seminars for a university, you would want to point up the financial success of what you did.

You might consider withholding any information that it would be better to discuss in person—your weak points, for example, or your past salaries (unless applicable in the circumstances), the names of persons you don't want bothered as references at this stage of your job hunt, or work you wouldn't want to do again, such as operating a switchboard or using certain mechanical skills. You can, if the story is true, tell about the time you saved your company some money, or developed a way to use time that otherwise would be wasted; but don't tell exactly *how* you did these things. You want your prospective employer to call you in for the full story.

To some, the functional résumé is basic and most useful. As its name indicates, the functional résumé is built around the *functions* of the job you are seeking. In preparing this type of résumé, you have to concentrate on the kind of job you want and the kinds you have held. You can begin by dividing and subdividing your experience in several sections. In each section you present what you have done in a particular field. If you are writing a résumé for an advertising manager, for example, you can divide your experience as follows: (a) in copy writing, describe the kinds of copy you wrote and the particular products or media for which you wrote; (b) in administration, describe its scope, and whether your experience as administrator was gained in the advertising department of some company or for some advertising agency; (c) in art, indicate the type of art work you have done, and whether you worked under supervision or independently; (d) in sales promotion, specify who employed you in that capacity.

Occupational Inventory For a Functional Résumé

NAME AND ADDRESS

Start by writing your name and address at one margin of the sheet and your telephone number at the other. Leave one blank line between your name and address, allowing your name to stand out. You may type this right at the margin or you may indent somewhat.

OCCUPATIONAL OBJECTIVES

This should be a clearly worded statement of the field in which you want to work. It is most important that you express yourself exactly here; you might find yourself in a position which, although it fits your qualifications, does not satisfy your ability completely or points you in the wrong direction. This statement should also tell the reader that you are not looking for just anything that might come along, so as to prevent your being offered just anything. Your overall objective may be stated generally, but the specific points in which you are interested must be stated precisely.

SUMMARY BY FUNCTIONS

If you are a technician, or an executive or a professional, and you are offering your services as a specialized employee, then the functional résumé can serve your purpose. Describe the major facets of your experience and background, such as:

(a) *Administration and management.* Indicate the kind of administration and management you were engaged in, and, using your background, state what you would like to do in the future.

(b) *Routine duties you performed.* What were these routine duties?

(c) *Technical accomplishments.* Give a functional description of any innovations you introduced or discoveries you made within your profession, and how such innovations and discoveries benefited your employers and increased your own knowledge and skill.

(d) *Supervision and management.* Describe the kind of equipment or personnel that was under your supervision and relate this description to any particular products developed. In this section, you attach your background in the company or companies for whom you worked. Also, indicate how successful you were in the performance of your administration or management of a department, division or branch, and whether the production or other work done was under your supervision.

(e) *Major fields of specialization preferred.* Specify the major fields in which you worked in the past. This will be related to the names of past employers, and will also denote which aspect of the work that you performed in the past you most enjoyed or preferred.

EXPERIENCE RECORD (OR HIGHLIGHTS)

Give the names and addresses of companies for which you worked, in reverse chronological order—that is, the most recent job first.

EDUCATION

Detailed information about your education is useful and important. Begin with your most advanced degree. If you have a master's, name the type of degree, school, its address, the year, your major subject and any pertinent facts connected with your attaining the degree, especially the titles and publication dates of your theses or dissertations, if any.

PROFESSIONAL AFFILIATIONS

Information about memberships in professional societies, including college fraternities, should be

142

presented here. State any special function, duty, title, or administrative post you may hold (or have held), and whether you are an active, honorary, professional or nonprofessional member.

OUTSIDE ACTIVITIES

This should include the names of all political, social, church, civic and community organizations in which you have participated actively. This information also tells the employment or personnel manager something about you in addition to your work history.

PERSONAL DATA

This is the same entry that is generally placed near the beginning of the résumé, but which we recommend you place here.
Date of birth (optional)
Marital status
Health
Date of last physical ex-
   amination
Height
Weight
Willing to relocate?
Will travel?

SALARY

Specify your salary range. On a separate piece of paper, list your salary history to submit on request.

REFERENCES

Submit on request. Collect letters of recommendation from past employers to have available when requested. Make duplicates so that you will not have to part with the originals.

Portfolio of Samples of the Functional Résumé

Advertising-Art Production Manager—Functional Résumé

RÉSUMÉ OF
>Billi J. Farris
>1301 Wabansia Avenue
>W.
>Chicago, IL 60622
>Date:
>Phone: (312)765-1239

OBJECTIVE
>To be placed in charge of the art department of a small advertising agency, where I can supervise the different stages of advertising-art production.

SUMMARY OF FUNCTIONAL EXPERIENCE
>Have extensive experience and responsibilities in production from layout to finish, including illustrations. As ad agency supervisor, did brochures, flyers, booklets, publicity ads, sales-presentation slide films and easel sales presentations. Have also done promotion pieces for educational and communications organizations.

WORK RECORD
>*Production Manager.* Aulick Advertising Corp., Chicago, IL. 19 . . . to 19 . . . In cooperation with my assistants, arranged to have the ads printed for publication or filmed for television use.

144

Advertising Copywriter. Blake, Hill Corp., Chicago, IL. 19 . . . to 19 . . . After studying the product and its potential customers, wrote copy aimed at the particular type of customers the advertiser sought to attract.

Advertising Research Supervisor. Ditmar, Myer & Co., Chicago, IL. 19 . . . to 19 . . . Studied the market for the product or service being sold. Did research in different facets of its possible uses, advantages and disadvantages, and compared the information about the product or service with that of the competitors.

EDUCATION

B.S. degree, Roosevelt University, Chicago, IL, 19 . . . Majored in business administration and advertising. Also took specialized courses in copywriting, illustration and layout at Chicago Institute of Art.

PROFESSIONAL MEMBERSHIPS

Advertising Federation of America (A.F.A.), New York, NY
International Advertising Association, New York, NY

PERSONAL DATA

Born: 7/22/19 . . .,
  Evanston, IL
Married, two children
Health: excellent
Height: 5'10"
Weight: 170 lbs.
Will relocate

SALARY

In the $25,000s plus fringe benefits and possibilities for promotion. (History of salaries available on request.)

REFERENCES

Available on request.

Commercial Artist—Functional Résumé

RÉSUMÉ OF
   Carla B. Landa
   300 W. 12th Street
   New York, NY 10014
   Date:
   Phone: (212)286-3979

OBJECTIVE

To be connected with the Production Department of an advertising agency, newspaper or book publisher. I have a good promotion and advertising sense, so that in my art work I know how to arouse and stimulate interest on the part of the reader in particular products, ideas or activities.

SUMMARY OF FUNCTIONAL EXPERIENCE

Concept of Commercial Art. Possess considerable insights and abilities in a number of the specialized areas of commercial advertising art. Can construct layouts that are in accord with the most current advertising ideas, with a view to best results.

Mechanics of Art Distribution. Am familiar with all the various drafting instruments, as well as brushes and pens needed in arranging and organizing a layout, and know the use of paste-ups as a basis for the copy to be used either in direct-mail advertising, or for some special graphic purposes.

Work as Accepted by Clients. Possess a good portfolio of illustrations that attests to the kind of job assignments I have had and on which I have worked as a free-lance artist. These free-lance job assignments

147

included illustrated brochures, book jackets, advertising and other promotion materials used in printed media.

WORK RECORD
Free-Lance Studio, 2 West 12th Street, New York, NY 10014, 19 . . . to present

TRAINING AND BACKGROUND
High school graduate, Richmond Hill High School, 46 Jackson St., Richmond Hill, NY 11418
Students' Art League, 801 Park Ave., New York, NY 10016

PERSONAL DATA
Born: 3/30/19 . . .
Single
Excellent health
Height: 5'5"
Weight: 120 lbs.
Willing to relocate

SALARY
Salary open to negotiation, in line with the responsibilities and the type of work expected.

REFERENCE AND PORTFOLIO
Available on request.

Dietitian—Functional Résumé

RÉSUMÉ OF
   Marjorie N. Snyder
   1139 Johnson N.
   St. Paul, MN 55413
   Date:
   Phone: (612)987-2345

OBJECTIVE
   To secure a position in private industry or in an institution where my years of experience as a dietitian can be used to function as a general supervisor or in one of the major branches of dietetics.

SUMMARY OF FUNCTIONAL EXPERIENCE
   Have had ten years of varied experience in the different branches of dietetics: administrative, clinical research, nutrition. My ability as an administrator was recognized where I worked and where I was asked to return at a better salary.

   Management Function. Can apply the principles of nutrition and administration to large-scale planning and preparation of meals in hospitals, schools and other large enterprises. Can supervise the service of meals; select, train and direct food-service supervisors and workers; and budget the purchase of food, equipment and supplies.

   Therapeutic Function. As a clinical dietitian, can plan diets and supervise the service of meals to meet the nutritional needs of patients in hospitals, nursing homes and clinics. Can supervise the preparation of meals according to individual needs, under the in-

149

structions of the medical team. Can also advise the patients' families with regard to dietary needs as prescribed by the doctors.

Research Function. As a research dietitian, can conduct, evaluate and interpret the findings of research to improve the nutritional level of both healthy and sick people. The research I engaged in related to nutritional needs of aging, chronically ill patients, and of space travelers.

Nutritionist Function. As a nutritionist, can counsel people of all ages, individually or in groups, with regard to maintaining and improving health through proper nutrition. This includes special diets, meal planning and preparation, and food budgeting and purchasing. Nutritionists in the public-health field are responsible for planning, developing, administering and coordinating nutrition programs and services as part of public-health programs.

WORK RECORD

Research Dietitian, General Foods Corp., White Plains, NY

Nutritionist, Health Dept., Nutrition Div., St. Paul, MN

Administrative Dietitian, Minnesota Medical Center, Minneapolis, MN

EDUCATION

B.S. degree, Cornell University, Home Economics College, Ithica, NY, 19 . . . Majored in food and nutrition; took such courses as institution management, chemistry, bacteriology, physiology and related courses. My internship lasted 12 months under the New York Hospital training program. All the academic as well as the internship courses were conducted under qualified dietitians and specialists in their fields.

PROFESSIONAL AFFILIATIONS
The American Dietetic Association, Chicago, IL

PERSONAL DATA
Born: 5/19/19 . . .
Yearly physical
Height: 5'6"
Weight: 120 lbs.
Wear glasses
Willing to relocate, if
position offers
opportunity for
teaching

SALARY
In the $20,000s plus benefits and teaching opportunity. History of salaries available.

REFERENCES
Available on request.

Fund Raiser—Functional Résumé

RÉSUMÉ OF
John G. Markowitz
315 East 71st St.
New York, NY 10021
Date:
Phone: (212)678-3542

SUMMARY OF EXPERIENCE
Experienced in the field of fund raising for nonprofit organizations. My duties consisted of contacting individuals and firms by telephone, in person or by other means, to solicit funds for hospitals, organizations engaged in health research, and so on. All the fund-raising projects with which I was connected in the last seven years were successful. In fact, four of these projects still require my services as a consultant for their annual fund-raising campaigns.

OBJECTIVE
To be employed in raising funds for a meritorious organization on a full-time, year-round basis. I require a salary plus a percentage of the total sums collected.

WORK RECORD
Fund-Raising Manager, New England Heart Society, New Haven, CT, 19 . . . to present. In this job I have been working in the Fund-Raising Division, which is a part of the public-relations activities of this nonprofit organization. I prepare news releases and supply a great deal of information suitable for use in the campaigns that are continually being carried on to

raise money for research in diseases of the heart and educate the public in the prevention of these diseases.

Public-Relations Assistant Manager, Misericordia Hospital, Stamford, CT, 19 . . . to 19 . . . As a member of the Public-Relations Department, was in charge of preparing and collecting information for publicity purposes, compiling and selecting mailing lists and issuing news releases. All these activities were part of the annual fund-raising campaign for the hospital. As public-relations assistant manager, it was part of my duties to consult with fund-raising specialists, for the better conduct of our campaigns. This position gave me a considerable background in the techniques of fund raising.

EDUCATIONAL BACKGROUND

B.A. in public relations, Boston University, Boston, MA, June 19 . . . Majored in English. Took courses in public relations and publicity, industrial relations, economics, sociology and philosophy. Was president of Delta Kappa Epsilon social fraternity. Elected to Pi Delta Epsilon, national honorary journalism fraternity. College was financed through earnings and family allowance.

GREW UP IN NEW YORK CITY

Father owns his own business. Attended New York City public schools; prepared for college at Forest Hills High School. Took part in sports. Member of school newspaper editorial staff.

PROFESSIONAL AFFILIATIONS

Public Relations Society of America, New York, NY
American Management Association, New York, NY
Industrial Publicity Association, New York, NY

PERSONAL INTERESTS
Enjoy playing tennis, swimming and reading.

OUTSIDE ACTIVITIES
Member of the Larchmont Country Club, Larchmont,
NY
Member of the University Club, New Haven, CT
Member of Stamford Athletic Club, Stamford, CT

PERSONAL DATA
Born: 9/6/19 . . .
Married, one child
Height: 5'10"
Weight: 165 lbs.
Will relocate and travel,
if position merits

SALARY
Salary and commission open to negotiation. History of
salaries available.

REFERENCES
Available on request

Human-Resources Executive—
Functional Résumé

RÉSUMÉ OF
Jane L. Nelson
80 Park Avenue
New York, NY 10016
Date:
Tel: (212)697-3536

OCCUPATIONAL OBJECTIVE
Position must be senior enough to help in implementing corporate personnel policies, and include reporting liaison between me and the compensation manager, the personnel managers in outlying locations,
and managers of employee relations and personnel
services. The major occupational functions should also
include implementing and monitoring affirmative
action programs, field recruiting, administering compensation programs and orienting line management
to the latest requirements and techniques in personnel.

INTERVIEWING AND RECRUITING
Currently employed as interviewer with a large engineering and contracting firm. This entails technical
and nontechnical interviewing and recruiting of male
applicants. After a few months with this firm, I was
placed in charge of male and female recruiting.
Prior employment includes two years with the Rush
Construction Company as the only employment interviewer (a staff of approximately 500), where I also
handled the administration of their group health
program. As associate personnel manager of the

American Health Organization in Philadelphia, PA, I interviewed and hired all clerical and secretarial personnel, and gave initial interviews to medical staff. This organization was new. It expanded from about 45 employees to over 400 while I was there, with the usual complement of interviews. Earlier, I had handled payroll, group health and employee counseling for a real-estate firm and for a large international airline.

CREATIVE ABILITY

I wrote an English script on tuberculosis for a health-education puppet show, which was translated into Spanish and was used with excellent results all over Central America and the Caribbean countries under the auspices of the American Health Organization. At the Colombian embassy in Washington, wrote a monthly "Economic Survey of the U.S.A." from material published in the leading U.S. newspapers, which was distributed among all Colombian embassies. I have written considerable newspaper advertising for recruiting purposes, as well as "Job Progress and Evaluation Reports" on personnel-job descriptions and interviews.

WORK RECORD

Assistant in Personnel Surveys and Office Interviewer, C.B. Technical Consulting Associates, New York, NY Among my duties was the search for specialized personnel for some of our customers.

Assistant Personnel Manager, Rush Construction Co., Dallas, TX

Assistant Personnel Manager, American Health Organization, Philadelphia, PA

156

Was in charge of preparation and promotion for recruiting and interviewing new employees.

News Letter Editor, Colombian embassy, Washington,
DC

EDUCATION
B.A., Temple University, Philadelphia, PA

PERSONAL DATA
Born: 19 . . ., Reading,
PA
Married
Height: 5'8"
Working knowledge of
Spanish

SALARY
Open in the $25,000s—no relocation. (History of
salaries available.)

REFERENCES
Available on request. (The above experience can be
documented by press clippings and official correspondence, and by personnel, statistical and economic
studies.)

Industrial Designer—Functional Résumé

RÉSUMÉ OF
   Jerome Hicks
   318 Pollock Ave.
   Los Angeles, CA 90018
   Date:
   Phone: (213)789-3452

OBJECTIVE
   To find a connection with a large manufacturer who already has a line of products on the market, and with whom my years of experience can be utilized for the production of ideas that are functionally necessary and not just experimental.

SUMMARY OF EXPERIENCE AND FUNCTIONS
   I am an industrial designer who combines talent with a knowledge of marketing, materials, machines and methods of production as they relate to products that can compete favorably with similar products on the market.
   Commercial Application of Design. The designer who can consider the immediate commercial value of a product usually prepares several sketches to submit to the advertising, marketing, sales and managerial personnel for an opinion and decision as to its manufacture.
   Basic Suitable Design. After a design has been selected, the next step is to make a final design or model, and to select the material to be used in the final product.
   Design for Consumer. Whether the product to be designed is large or small, first consideration must be

given to the consumer of the product, before the attempt to manufacture. Appearance and ease of manufacture are not always prime considerations in the final choice.

WORK RECORD

19...–19...
Household Implements and Supplies Corp., Riverside, CA
Basic Industrial Designer

19...–19...
Metal Furniture Mfg. Co., Compton, CA
Office-Equipment Designer

19...–19...
Plastics Mfg. Corp., Anaheim, CA
Plastic-Products Designer

EDUCATION

B.S. in industrial design, Armstrong College, Los Angeles, CA, June 19... The importance of this course lay in the fact that it stressed equally the necessity of an art background and the technical aspects of industrial design. Since industrial designers must cooperate with engineers and other staff members, this course also emphasized the importance of being able to work and communicate with others.

PROFESSIONAL ACCOMPLISHMENTS

A number of designs were accepted before my graduation, by Industrial Designers, for whom I worked on a part-time basis.

PROFESSIONAL AFFILIATIONS

Industrial Designers Society of America, McLean, VA

PERSONAL DATA
   Born: 5/19/19...
   Good health
   Height: 5'7"
   Weight: 155 lbs.
   Willing to relocate, if
       position merits

SALARY
   In the $20,000s with good benefits. History of salaries
   available.

REFERENCES
   Character and professional references available, as
   well as a rather complete and large portfolio of
   designs that were used in the last five years.

Landscape Architect—Functional Résumé

RÉSUMÉ OF
Raymond J. Novarro
1206 American Ave. S.
Philadelphia, PA 19147
Date:
Phone: (215)567-3456

OBJECTIVE

To secure employment as a full-landscape architect, with a local or state urban development or a large construction developer that needs the services of an experienced landscape architect. Seek opportunity with a firm that can offer possibilities of advancement.

SUMMARY OF FUNCTIONAL EXPERIENCE

Have the education and experience as a landscape architect to complete any project in my field. First, study the nature and purpose of the commercial, institutional or housing complex involved; consult with the building architect and engineers; determine funds available for the job; consider the various types of surrounding buildings. Then, make maps of the site itself, noting slope of land and position of existing buildings and trees. Also determine which sections will be sunny or shady at different times of the day, as well as composition of the soil, existing utilities and many other factors affecting the landscape's design. After assembling this data, draw plans for development of the site. Finally, outline in detail the methods for construction of special features, and compile list of building materials, flowering and other plant life needed to produce artistic color combinations; provide

161

for maximum health of plants, and allow for growth so that future extension of limbs of trees do not interfere with other trees.

Artistic Beautification. Have complete understanding of architectural and landscape design, of roads, fountains, benches; can distribute shade trees and floral groupings to produce an attractive and colorful setting that is also functional and aesthetically appealing.

Botanical Background. Have knowledge of the botany of plants and shrubs, and of horticulture and evaluation of plants as to their resistance to disease. Aware of the most successful combinations for effective development and prolonged life, allowing for future extension of limbs so that one tree does not interfere with another.

Business and Development Expertise. Can offer surveys, construction requirements, contracts and specifications and cost estimates, and can supervise general business procedures concerning assignments.

WORK RECORD

Landscape Contractor's Supervisor, 19 . . . to 19 . . ., Philadelphia Park Development Department, Philadelphia, PA

Junior Landscape Engineer, 19 . . . to 19 . . ., Knoll, Key Architects, Inc., Pittsburgh, PA

Designer Supervisor, 19 . . . to 19 . . ., Landscape Engineers, Inc., Philadelphia, PA

EDUCATION

B.S. in landscape engineering, June 19 . . ., Pennsylvania State University, PA

LICENSES

Hold licenses for landscape architect in the states of Pennsylvania and New Jersey.

PROFESSIONAL MEMBERSHIP
   American Society of Landscape Architecture, Inc., Mc-
   Lean, VA

PERSONAL DATA
   Born: 6/18/19 . . .
   Married, no children
   Good health
   Height: 5'10"
   Weight: 170 lbs.
   Willing to relocate if
      there is reciprocity in
      the licensure with the
      state of Pennsylvania.

SALARY
   In the $25,000s, plus expenses of relocation and
   fringe benefits. (History of salaries available.)

REFERENCES
   Good professional and character references available
   on request.

Nurse, Registered—Functional Résumé

RÉSUMÉ OF
Helen T. Goltermann_
311 East 79th Street
New York, NY 10036
Date:
Phone: (212)768-3578

OBJECTIVE

To continue in the practice of my profession in a hospital where supervision of new personnel is needed, and where I can be of constructive help in accordance with my background, training and experience.

SUMMARY OF FUNCTIONAL EXPERIENCE

Hospital Nursing. Am qualified to provide skilled nursing care and to carry out doctor's instructions in regard to medical care of patient. Can supervise practical nurses, aides and similar personnel. Have had to exercise responsible judgment in such areas as postsurgery patients, those in the recovery stage after suffering a stroke, and working with the proper medicines ordered by the doctors, as well as the therapy involved.

Public-Health Nursing. Have been connected with public-health in division that was in charge of helping patients at home or in out-patient clinics, and children at school. When visiting patients at home, have instructed them and their families as to the proper care necessary, the proper administration of medicines and other aspects of care as prescribed by the doctor. Have gained much experience in instructing special patients or groups of patients as to proper diet; and when necessary, had the skill to immunize or inoculate patients in accordance with orders of the doctor.

Industrial Nursing. In this area, worked in a manufacturing firm on Long Island, where the duties were varied and where I had to display a great deal of skill in observing patients while providing the necessary nursing care, and was able to lay particular stress on the importance of preventing ill health and fostering good health. Treated minor injuries and illnesses at the place of employment, provided nursing care and arranged for further medical care where needed. Took special care with examinations as required and performed inoculations and other duties as ordered by the physician.

WORK RECORD

Columbia Presbyterian Medical Center, New York, NY 10032. 19 . . . to present

Bellevue Hospital, New York, NY 10016. 19 . . . to 19 . . .

Montefiore Hospital & Medical Center, Bronx, NY 10467. 19 . . . to 19 . . .

QUALIFICATIONS THROUGH TRAINING

After graduating from George Washington High School, New York, NY, attended the Cornell School of Nursing, in New York. My regular license is from New York State. I also have rehabilitation licenses in nursing for the District of Columbia, Virginia, Florida and Illinois.

MEMBERSHIP

American Nurses Association, Kansas City, KS

SALARY

Open to negotiation, according to duties and responsibilities. History of salaries available on request.

REFERENCES

Available on request.

Overseas Production Manager—Functional Résumé

RÉSUMÉ OF
William V. Gig
20 Court Street
Brooklyn, NY 11224
Date:
Phone: (212)678-3579

OBJECTIVE

As a highly skilled and experienced professional I am seeking a post as international project manager with a worldwide leader in the manufacture of chemicals and pharmaceuticals—a post that offers a challenging opportunity and responsibility. Prefer the home base in the United States with not more than 25% traveling incidental to the duties.

CONTRACTS, AGENCIES, SUBSIDIARIES

Specialist in commercial and industrial problems and in domestic and foreign-government contract negotiations. Am familiar with establishment of new branches in the United States or foreign countries; can open up new agencies and organize new subsidiaries, together with licensing negotiations and programming new projects. Skilled in negotiating with authorities; resourceful in finding investment opportunities. Qualified to supervise studies, surveys, pilot projects, and to report for action to top management.

KNOWLEDGE OF ECONOMIC AND POLITICAL CONDITIONS

Intimate knowledge of economic and political conditions in the United States as well as in foreign

167

countries—a knowledge that is essential to the conduct of business. Possess the ability to compare the tax situation in the United States with that in foreign countries where the company has already established business, or is planning to do so through subsidiaries or affiliates. The problems incidental to taxation, as well as those related to personnel payments and hiring, are important factors to be considered when planning for profits in the future.

WORK RECORD

Supervisor of Foreign Operations, 19 . . . to 19 . . ., Abbott Laboratories, North Chicago, IL

Foreign Operations Director, 19 . . . to 19 . . ., IMC Chemical Group, Inc., Boston, MA

KNOWLEDGE OF LANGUAGES

Working knowledge of Spanish. Traveled throughout South and Central America, Mexico, Orient.

MEMBERSHIPS AND AFFILIATIONS

Past President, Lions Club
U.S. Chamber of Commerce, Washington, DC
Latin American Chamber of Commerce, New York, NY
Drive Director, Community Chest

PERSONAL DATA

Married, 2 children
Good health
Height: 5'9"
Weight: 210 lbs.

SALARY

In the $30,000s plus regular executive fringe benefits, etc. (History of salaries to be presented in a possible interview.)

REFERENCES

Available on request. Excellent top-level business, government and personal references.

Radiology Technician—Functional Résumé

RÉSUMÉ OF
> Nathan O. Miller (ARRT)
> 2230 L Street, N.W.
> Washington, DC 20037
> Date:
> Phone: (202)987-3675

OBJECTIVE
> Am anxious to make a connection with a medical center or official agency where I can work as a technologist in the field of nuclear medicine, in which radioactive isotopes are used to diagnose and treat disease. Am ambitious to expand my knowledge in the administration of prescribed radioisotopes and in the operation of special equipment for tracing and measuring radioactivity.

SUMMARY OF FUNCTIONAL EXPERIENCE
> Have a complete knowledge of X-ray equipment as used in hospitals and clinics. Know exactly how to prepare solutions or chemical mixtures, such as barium salts, and can explain to the patient the reasons for using these. Am well informed as to the necessary security required in protecting the patient, as well as myself, from radiation in therapy as prescribed by the doctor. I have always been particularly careful in keeping records in connection with all radiotherapy treatments. All told, I have five years of experience.

WORK RECORD
> *Radiology Technologist*, Columbia Hospital, 2425 L St., N.W., Washington, DC, 19 . . . to 19 . . .

170

Radiology Technologist, George Washington University Medical Center, Washington, DC, 19 . . . to 19 . . .

Assistant Radiology Technologist, Washington Hospital Center, Washington, DC, 19 . . . to 19 . . .

TRAINING AND MILITARY SERVICE

Graduated from Benjamin Franklin High School, Baltimore, MD. After graduating, joined the Army for two years. Took courses for X-ray specialist (91P). This course took 19 weeks. Learned how to operate X-ray equipment, to take radiographs, and to assist radiologists in the treatment prescribed. After I left the Army, attended Louis Brandeis Junior College in Baltimore, MD. This course is approved by the American Medical Association. It lasted 24 months, and the cost was met under the G.I. educational program.

MEMBERSHIP

American Registry of Radiology Technologists, Minneapolis, MN

The American Society of Radiology Technologists, Chicago, IL

SALARY

In the $16,000s, open to negotiation in accordance with the duties and responsibilities, and the fringe benefits applicable for this type of hazardous work.

REFERENCES

Dr. William H. Hinkley, Georgetown Medical Center, Washington, DC 20005

Dr. Alice B. Hopkins, Washington Hospital, Washington, DC 20036

Mr. Robert H. Harris, (ARRT) General Supervisor of the Radiology Department, Columbia Hospital, Washington. DC 20023

Sales-Promotion Manager—
Functional Résumé

RÉSUMÉ OF
  Jack E. Lands
  1010 North Dearborn
  Chicago, IL 60611
  Date:
  Phone: (312)435-3388

OBJECTIVE
  To secure a position in the capacity of sales-promotion
  manager whose direct responsibility would be to the
  president or the executive vice-president, and where
  proven ability and experience in sales promotion,
  marketing, merchandising, public relations and publicity would be needed and appreciated.

SUMMARY OF FUNCTIONAL EXPERIENCE
  Sales and Merchandise. Contributed toward annual
    sales of intangibles that amounted to about
    $3,500,000. Was responsible for developing new
    markets and introducing new products to the con-
    sumer. Broad experience in the sale of both tangible
    and intangible products and services. Sold adver-
    tising to companies, distributors, agencies and im-
    porters, and assisted in developing advertising and
    marketing campaigns for products; also developed
    sales for military installations. Represented leading
    daily newspapers in the United States and Canada
    for national advertising campaigns, sales promo-
    tion and public relations. Trained and supervised
    salesmen. Specialized in new business develop-

ment. Complete understanding of sales and merchandising patterns.

Marketing and Promotion. Through direct contact with manufacturers, retailers, brokers and regional sales offices of major manufacturers and marketing firms, have acquired a thorough knowledge of all aspects of sales and distribution. Have been troubleshooter in the retail and wholesale grocery and drug trade for a national marketer. Worked with point-of-purchase materials, made arrangements for store displays and created merchandising programs, sales letters, brochures and other sales aids for integrated promotion programs. Conducted various types of consumer interviews and market surveys for major national companies and processed, evaluated and applied necessary data.

Public Relations and Publicity. Have been representative of companies at trade shows, conventions and various business functions. Responsible for maintaining good business relationships between company and clients. Coordinated liaison between newspapers to obtain support for advertisers by means of press releases, photos and news stories. Sponsored the showing of promotional films.

WORK RECORD

Sales Assistant. Alden Press, Inc., Arlington Heights, IL. 19 . . . to present

Salesman. Altra Corp, Elk Grove Village, IL. 19 . . . to 19 . . .

Marketing and Merchandising Representative, Amedoo, Inc., Springfield, IL. 19 . . . to 19 . . .

EDUCATION

Forest Park College, Forest Park, IL. B.S. in business

administration, with minor in communications. Certified to teach these subjects.

Courses in marketing and public relations at Northwestern University, Chicago, IL

Jones High School, Chicago, IL

SALARY

In the $25,000s, open to negotiation. History of salaries available.

REFERENCES

Available on request.

TV and Radio Announcer—
Functional Résumé

RÉSUMÉ OF
> Conrad H. Hoppe
> 2201 Kirkland Ave., S.
> Chicago, IL 60623
> Date:
> Phone: (312)678-3452

OBJECTIVE
> To be connected with national hookup TV stations, where my experience as announcer, anchor man or director of specials could be utilized to mutual advantage.

SUMMARY OF FUNCTIONAL EXPERIENCE
> *Announcer.* In this capacity, introduced programs, guest and musical selections, and conducted a great many commercial TV and radio programs. While many of the programs related to sports and the weather, my real forte is as news announcer. Whenever necessary, I was able to write my own scripts based on my own research.
>
> *Business and Sales.* In the area of business management, can handle accounting, publicity, public relations and personnel matters as the job would require. Since TV and radio depend on good sponsors, have engaged in selling advertising to agencies and to other buyers. Am considered to have special ability in observing the psychological characteristics of the announcer, along with the demands of the particular area served.
>
> *Programming Selections.* Since I have come up through the ranks, I am familiar with the various aspects of

the field of TV and radio, especially as regards selecting personnel and arranging schedules. Understand and get along well with actors, comedians, singers and other entertainers that need to be hired for particular programs, or for special assignments.

WORK RECORD

WCBS, Chicago, IL. I substituted for personnel absent for whatever reason, in preparing scripts regarding sports and the weather, and as anchor man for the news.

WNEC, Oklahoma City, OK. This is a small television station, so that my duties were varied. When I left the station it had increased its volume of business by more than 75%.

WTAB, Houston, TX. As a disc jockey and salesman of programs, I had to ad-lib a large part of my comments, without reference to script.

EDUCATION

B.A. degree in Liberal Arts, Brown University, RI, June 19 . . . Took a number of courses in radio and television, in addition to the regular courses required for the degree. Gained experience and an understanding of the field by helping in the radio station of the campus, and by engaging in radio and television work during the summers.

PERSONAL DATA

Born: 3/30/19 . . .
Married
Height: 6'1"
Weight: 165 lbs.

E.C.C. radiotelephone
  third-class operator
  license.
Free-lance lecturer at
  colleges
Will relocate

SALARY

Open to negotiation in accordance with the duties.
History of salaries available.

REFERENCES

Available on request.

———————————————————————————————

8

Preparation of the Modern Analytical Résumé

How to Prepare a Modern Analytical Résumé

The *modern analytical résumé* is somewhat more complex than the functional résumé because it presents the necessary information in greater detail. It can be said that the modern analytical résumé offers the prospective employer or the interviewer a broader base from which to judge the qualifications of the applicant. It is favored by professionals, executives or highly specialized workers. For those who possess leadership qualities and can supervise others, who enjoy thinking about and solving problems, who like educational work and who are adept at figures, the modern analytical résumé should be their choice.

In preparing the final draft of your résumé, it isn't necessary to use every item that follows. You can select those which apply to you particularly. For example, you may know a foreign language—a valuable asset in your field of endeavor, while someone else might consider it of no importance in his field of endeavor. Or, conversely, you might not want to say anything about your clerical ability, thinking that there is no need for it in your field. The instructions given here are intended to provide all possible entries for your personal résumé.

The modern analytical résumé is a combination of the better or more outstanding qualities of the three preceding types of résumés. It includes all the advantages of what used to be known as the Harvard Résumé; that is, it analyzes, step by step, the more essential aspects of your business profile.

The modern analytical résumé permits you to stress the major areas of skill that are pertinent aspects of your work, as these relate to the position you are seeking. It supplies the employer with a great many details that would not be necessary to point out in jobs that can be covered in a basic, chronological or functional résumé. Also, it presents the material in more logical sequence than in the functional résumé and highlights the importance of each job held in each company.

In the modern analytical résumé you are given the opportunity to emphasize the qualifications for the job you are aiming at, as well as to highlight your particular skills and abilities. In addition, the modern analytical résumé allows you to concentrate on the kinds of work you did and the jobs you held in the past.

For example, an engineer can arrange his modern analytical résumé according to jobs worked on, presenting each as a project in problem-and-solution form. This type of résumé also permits the applicant to indicate and comment on the growth achieved with each job experience. It presents ascending steps and the progress made, as reflected in the different jobs held or duties performed. Because the modern analytical résumé is so very comprehensive, it offers the applicant an opportunity to submit supplemental information in a letter accompanying the résumé. Needless to say, personality, character and potential ability are revealed in these, and very often they play a major role in the best outcome for the applicant.

Apart from the advantages indicated above, the modern analytical résumé is particularly suited for a college graduate who has become a corporate lawyer, president of a company, marketing executive or any other post that can be classified as in the top management level.

So comprehensive is the modern analytical résumé in the opportunity it offers for occupational and self-revelation, that it also provides scope for answering questions that the interviewer may ask.

In preparing your modern analytical résumé, try to be as complete as possible in the information you present. It will serve you best if you do this.

Occupational Inventory for a Modern Analytical Résumé

NAME AND ADDRESS
Place your name and address on one side and your telephone number on the other.

SUMMARY OF EXPERIENCE
In 50 to 100 words summarize all the experience you have gained in the different positions you have held up to the present. This summary will provide the reader with an almost immediate idea as to whether you are the person to fill the job.

OCCUPATIONAL OBJECTIVE
In a sentence or two, name your field of specialization, or fields related to it, and the position you prefer. For example, an occupational objective

might be "to be associated with a growing, internationally oriented firm in the field of marketing or investment."

EXPERIENCE HIGHLIGHTS

Your previous experience may be the determining factor as to whether or not you are hired.

Give the name and location of the company (or companies) you were with, the title of your position there, the length of your employment. Describe your duties, pointing out those aspects of the work that might fit in with the job you now seek. If you are looking for a job in public relations or personnel, for example, you might explain your former jobs. If you are applying for a position as export manager, explain your sales experience and how it has helped you in the ability to deal with customers, to talk on the telephone, to write letters and to use the general principles of sales psychology.

EDUCATION

Give the details of your education and training, from high school on—the name and location of each school, the dates of your attendance and the dates of your graduation. Include the name of your curriculum or program, and the titles of any courses that had special relevance to the work you now seek.

EARLY BACKGROUND

Employers generally want this information because it rounds out the picture of the whole person. Here you can tell something of your history as a child: the environmental and educational factors, including after-school activities or occupations that helped to form the adult you now are.

PROFESSIONAL AFFILIATIONS AND LICENSES YOU HOLD

Information about memberships in professional societies should be presented here. State any special functions, duties, titles or administrative posts you have held or hold, and whether you are an active, honorary, professional or nonprofessional member.

If you work in a field that requires licensing from local, state or federal authorities, state those you have.

PERSONAL RECOGNITION

State the titles, publishers and dates of printing of all articles, papers, theses or books you have written. Employers like to have what is called "literary visibility" about their employees. Provide similar information in the scientific, technical or political fields.

CLUBS AND FRATERNITIES

This should include the names of all political, social, church, civic and community organizations in which you participate actively. This information also tells the employer or personnel recruiter something about you apart from your work history.

KNOWLEDGE OF FOREIGN LANGUAGE(S)

Many companies, with their interests abroad through exports, foreign investments and overseas branches, have an increasing demand for employees who speak another language fluently. List the language(s) you can speak fluently, but do not assume that any high school or college courses in a language can be regarded as giving you fluency. You either know a language fluently or you do not. Personnel people will almost certainly have you take a test in the foreign language. Failure in this test can be held against you. Therefore, honesty is the best policy when you state how well you read, write and speak another language.

OUTSIDE ACTIVITIES

One young lady, interviewed for a secretarial position, was puzzled when asked if she collected coins or stamps. What could the question possibly have to do with her skills and competence as a secretary? Actually, it might reveal more about her interests and background than a series of more routine questions. An interest in stamps shows that a person enjoys handling small details. An active pursuit of such a hobby can sharpen a person's sensitivity to fine distinctions and subtleties of arrangement.

Obviously we don't all want to be philatelists or numismatists. But it's important not to overlook the value of hobbies and extracurricular activities in selling yourself to a potential employer. The books and magazines you read, the games you enjoy and the things you collect can all be positive comments on your character and personality. An employer who knows that you participate in extracurricular activities, welfare-organization work or community projects knows that you are willing to work to accomplish things even when it is not required of you or when there is no financial reward. If you have been chairman of a committee, president of your class or captain of an athletic team, you have had practice in leadership that will make you a better candidate for an executive position. If you were advertising manager of your school paper or yearbook, the experience may prove valuable when you look for a job in public relations.

EMPLOYMENT INFORMATION

The following should be included under Employment Information:

When you are available for employment
If you are working now
When it will be most convenient for you to be interviewed
Whether or not you are willing to relocate within the United States
Whether or not you are willing to make a complete change and relocate in a foreign country
If you are willing or not to travel, and for what part of your time
If you have traveled—where and when

PERSONAL DATA

This entry should include information on the following:

Date of birth
Citizenship
Birthplace
Whether single or married
Number of children
Height
Physical limitations
Weight
State of health
Willing to relocate

SALARY

Specify your salary range. (On a separate piece of paper, list your salary history to submit on request.)

REFERENCES

An employer is almost certain to ask you for references as a check on your character and ability. You should have ready the names, addresses and telephone numbers of three to five people who know you well. The best references are from people who know your work—recommendations from friends or acquaintances on a purely social basis do not carry much weight. Of course, it is only polite to get advance permission from people you wish to use as references.

Portfolio of Samples of Modern Analytical Résumé

Accountant, Management—Modern Analytical Résumé

RÉSUMÉ OF
> Robert B. Hess
> 15 Church Hill Dr.
> Atlanta, GA 30338
> Date:
> Phone: (404)568-7231

SUMMARY OF EXPERIENCE

Seven years of experience in performing a variety of accounting and financial duties for several large companies in Georgia. Have served as troubleshooter when necessary, undertaken investigative and problem-solving assignments and engaged in consulting department. To avoid errors and difficulties, have supervised the daily work of accounting personnel.

OCCUPATIONAL OBJECTIVE

To work as chief accountant or supervisor in the accounting department of a large company where my experience in financial analysis and in auditing accounting systems will contribute to the overall control and operation of the department.

19 . . . to present
National Chemical Corp.
Atlanta, GA

Assistant Corporate Accountant. All my managerial responsibilities for this firm stem from my strong accounting background. Am responsible for such aspects of the work as cost accounting, corporate financial statements, tax accounting, cost control and analysis, billings and collections. I am thoroughly familiar with cash-flow management and budgets, and planning in these areas.

19 . . . to 19 . . .
Georgia Refining Corp.
Atlanta, GA

Management Accountant. This position required review of financial reports, including appropriate research, in addition to overseeing computer-terminal time-sharing applications. Included among the responsibilities were consolidations, F.A.S.B. and S.E.C. reporting and other special projects.

19 . . . to 19 . . .
Columbia Southern Manufacturing Co.
Atlanta, GA

Senior Accountant. Supervised a staff of 25 accountants. Apart from the duties of supervision, served as one of the financial officers during a period of expansion within the company. Was responsible for all the necessary financing to provide for expansion projects. Was directly responsible to the President and the Finance Committee of the Board of Directors for the entire financial program, including accounting statements, taxes and credits.

EDUCATIONAL BACKGROUND

> *Degree of Master in Business Administration* from University of Atlanta, School of Business, Atlanta, GA, June 19... The program of studies was pursued with a view to obtaining a broad background in advanced accounting and finance.

> *B.S. Degree in Commerce, cum laude,* June 19... Majored in accounting and finance, including economics, industrial organization, computing and programming. Member of Mathematics Club. Played scholastic basketball. Expenses partially financed through scholarships, summer work and financial help from home.

EARLY BACKGROUND

> *Grew up in Atlanta, GA.* Father an engineer with I.B.M. Attended publc schools and prepared for college at Abraham Lincoln High School. Member of the basketball team and the student council.

MILITARY SERVICE

> Joined the U.S. Army following graduation from high school. While in the Army took an 11-week course in computer programming (74F) under which I received instruction in analytical mathematics, investigative operations regarding personnel, finance, medical matters, data communication and intelligence, to help in developing ADP procedures and techniques.

PROFESSIONAL LICENSE

> Certified Public Accountant, Georgia, 19...

PROFESSIONAL MEMBERSHIPS

> American Accounting Association, New York, NY
> National Association of Cost Accountants (N.A.A.) New York, NY
> Management Accounting Society, New York, NY

PERSONAL DATA

Age, 38. Married, 2 children. Height, 6'0". Weight, 181 lbs. Good health. Last physical, 19 . . . Willing to relocate.

SALARY

In the $30,000s plus full benefits package and promotion opportunities based on performance. (History of salaries available.)

REFERENCES

Personal and professional on request.

Administrative Assistant—Modern Analytical Résumé

RÉSUMÉ OF

Natalie H. Williams
4710 Charles Terrace
Philadelphia, PA 19125
Date:
Phone: (215)345-6523

SUMMARY OF EXPERIENCE

Varied experience as secretary to the president of corporation and with nonprofit organizations and business associations. Duties have included typing (70 w.p.m.), light stenography, own correspondence, supervision of office personnel and planning and coordinating special events. Have prepared copy for brochures, promotional letters and publicity releases. Good background as paralegal aide. Organization ability. Detail-oriented.

OCCUPATIONAL OBJECTIVE

To secure the position of Administrative Assistant. Good candidate for research or administrative aid in financial or legal setting. Eager to apply this knowledge in a challenging position.

WORK-RECORD ANALYSIS

19 . . . to 19 . . .

Kenny, Wilson Corp.

Philadelphia, PA

Administrative Assistant. Worked closely with several members of the professional staff. The duties included filing, routing mail, answering letters, doing statistical research, typing the results in clear form and writing reports.

19 . . . to 19 . . .
Philadelphia Reference Publications, Inc.
Philadelphia, PA
Executive Secretary. In general, relieved my immediate superiors of routine duties so that they could work on more important matters. My duties varied greatly in different directions and my responsibilities increased. Left because I needed a better income.

19 . . . to 19 . . .
Silber & Harriman Corp.
Philadelphia, PA
Secretary. Was hired as secretary-stenographer to take dictation and to help in other secretarial duties. After a few weeks took more difficult dictation and was placed in charge of more responsible duties. Was present at all staff meetings and reported all the proceedings.

EDUCATIONAL BACKGROUND
Grew up in Haddonfield, NJ, where my father was schoolteacher. After high school graduation attended Katherine Gibbs Business School, in Montclair, NJ. Took their regular two-year secretarial course.

PERSONAL INTERESTS
Greatly interested in politics, and in welfare projects or programs such as Community Fund and Red Cross.

SALARY
Open to negotiation, according to duties and fringe benefits offered.

REFERENCES
Available on request.

Advertising Manager—
Modern Analytical Résumé

RÉSUMÉ OF

James T. Clarkson
161 Engert Avenue
Brooklyn, NY 11222
Date:
Phone: (212)768-7698

SUMMARY OF EXPERIENCE

Directed the advertising program of the business for which I worked. I helped to determine the size of the advertising budget, the type of ads and media to be used and the advertising agency, if any, that was employed. Worked closely with the account executives assigned to our firm. Possess extensive knowledge of how to prepare pamphlets, brochures, or other materials designed to promote the firm's products and services.

My work always required imagination and creativity. I get along very well with people and can sell ideas.

OCCUPATIONAL OBJECTIVE

To provide a corporation with an advertising manager who has ability in the wholesale and retail business, and who also possesses the background and experience to produce quality ads in as short a time as possible.

WORK-RECORD ANALYSIS

19 . . . to 19 . . .
American Duplicating Corp.
New York, NY
Advertising Sales-Promotion Manager. Worked closely

with the advertising manager and supervised the research department to provide sales support. Position involved marketing strategy, budgeting and execution of all advertising production projects.

19 . . . to 19 . . .
Jones & Jones Advertising Co.
New York, NY
Advertising Production Manager. In this position I had to rely on my technical knowledge of all major reproduction processes, and on my keen color sense and thorough knowledge of all art preparation. Other duties involved extensive purchasing and sales promotion, and drew on my ability to determine cost-saving specifications and to establish exacting and meaningful production schedules.

19 . . . to 19 . . .
AFA Advertising Corp.
New York, NY
Manager of Advertising Sales Promotion. As the manager of advertising sales promotion and customer relations, had to do substantial marketing of instruments in the capital equipment range of electronic and electro-optical systems. Familiarized myself with all methods commonly used in the promotion of this type of product in trade journals and through advertising, commercial exhibits, direct mail, public relations and other forms of promotion.

EDUCATIONAL BACKGROUND
Bachelor of Business Administration, 19 . . ., University of the City of New York, New York, NY. Majored in advertising, psychology; concentrated on English, sociology, personnel. Active in athletics. Served on student council. Expenses financed through earnings and family funds.

EARLY BACKGROUND

Grew up in Larchmont, NY. Father an executive of Borden Co. Attended public schools in Westchester, NY; prepared for college at Yonkers High School, Yonkers, NY. Graduated *cum laude* with class of 175 in 19 . . .

PROFESSIONAL MEMBERSHIPS

Advertising Federation of America (A.F.A.), New York, NY

International Advertising Association, New York, NY

Chamber of Commerce of New York, New York, NY

OUTSIDE ACTIVITIES

Very active in the Job-Finding Forum for the Handicapped, New York, NY.

Head company's annual Red Cross drive.

Interested in national and local politics.

PERSONAL INTERESTS

Golf and gardening during weekends. Reading technical literature.

PERSONAL DATA

Born: 6/7/19 . . .
Married, 2 children
Good health
Height: 5'9"
Weight: 172 lbs.
Willing to relocate

SALARY

In the $30,000s, with fringe benefits and good opportunities for promotion. (History of salaries available.)

REFERENCES

Available on request.

Aeronautical Engineer—Modern Analytical Résumé

RÉSUMÉ OF
Lloyd F. Harston
240 W. 21st Street
Rockford, IL 61105
Date:
Tel: (312)967-4861

SUMMARY OF EXPERIENCE

Worked on all types of aircraft and spacecraft including missiles, rockets, military and commercial planes. Specialized in passenger planes from the initial planning and design to the final assembly and testing.

OCCUPATIONAL OBJECTIVE

To be associated with a multinational company as an aeronautical engineer, where my education and ability will lead to a responsible position.

WORK-RECORD ANALYSIS

19 . . . to present
National Aeronautics & Space Administration
Rockford, IL

Section Manager. Manage all test operations including propulsion, electrical and hydraulic tests in Aviation Division, as well as research, development and production. Manage design of all test equipment and new test-lab designs. Supervise up to 150 professional and nonprofessional people and manage $70,000 budget plus capital equipment budget.

19 . . . to 19 . . .

National Aeronautics & Space Administration
Houston, TX

Branch Head for both ground and flight tests required to develop Apollo spacecraft. Managed support contractor programs. Led in defining software required in Apollo program, and defined program-office role in operation at Manned Spacecraft Center.

19 . . . to 19 . . .

Spacecraft Manager and Assistant Branch Head. Managed N.A.S.A. and contractor efforts to define mission, manufacture and checkout of first Apollo spacecraft. Spacecraft manager of first Apollo spacecraft. Established P.E.R.T. net.

19 . . . to 19 . . .

Acting Chief, Apollo Command- and Service-Module Test. Determined spacecraft instrumentation requirements. Assigned and supervised project engineers. Was lead in developing Apollo project development plan, and editor, data-analysis and report-team manager for first Apollo flight-test report.

EDUCATIONAL BACKGROUND

B.E. Degree in Aeronautical Engineering, Rensselaer Polytechnic Institute, Troy, NY, June 19 . . . Majored in aircraft-engine design, minored in rotary-wing aircraft. Program arranged primarily to provide thorough training in this specialized field. Preliminary study in basic aspects of arts and sciences was required. Courses in elementary aeronautics, aircraft performance and stability, aircraft structures, aircraft design, aircraft components, advanced aerodynamics. Member of the Technical Club. Active in college athletics, especially intramural tennis and football.

198

Member of Mathematics Society. Thesis on "Aeronautical Engineering in Today's Transportation" was very well received by my advisors and other faculty members. Education financed with own funds and family allowances.

MILITARY SERVICE
U.S. Army, 19...–19... Served in U.S. and Europe as radio technician. Outstanding letters of commendation from superiors. Honorably discharged; not in reserves.

PROFESSIONAL MEMBERSHIP
National Aeronautic Association (N.A.A.), Washington, DC

EARLY BACKGROUND
Grew up in New York City, son of mechanical engineer with Pan American Airways. Attended public schools; prepared for college at De Witt Clinton High School, N.Y.C., graduated 19... Played intramural football. Member of library team, Science Club. Joined U.S. Army on graduation, 19...

PERSONAL INTERESTS
Enjoy swimming and tennis as time allows, reading technical literature on aviation, bowling and social activities.

OUTSIDE ACTIVITIES
McBurney Y.M.C.A., Rockford, IL
Member of the Rockford Country Club

PERSONAL DATA
Born: 3/17/19 . . .
Single
Height: 5'9"
Weight: 170 lbs.
Willing to relocate

SALARY
Open to negotiation.

REFERENCES
References available on request.

Aircraft Pilot—Modern Analytical Résumé

RÉSUMÉ OF

Gary M. Hudson
319 Roosevelt Avenue
Huntington, NY 11743
Date:
Phone: (516)456-6732

SUMMARY OF EXPERIENCE

Experienced pilot from small- to large-schedule planes. Able to perform all the duties incident to operating the controls, and other necessary tasks for getting the craft into air, keeping it on course and landing safely. Able to examine airframe, engines and operating equipment to insure that repairs are made according to specifications, and to certify worthiness of aircraft. Can test tightness of airframe connections with handtools, especially as to the fitness of all parts. Capable of taking responsibility for the safety of passengers and cargo. Experienced in the supervision of all personnel needed in the operation and services offered in the aircraft. Have all the required licensing and physical fitness for controlling and supervising aircraft and air-transportation service. Long experience in night and instrument flying.

OCCUPATIONAL OBJECTIVE

To secure a position as chief captain supervisor in one of the international airlines where I will be placed in charge of international aircraft scheduling, maintenance and flight procedures. Also desire to do a certain amount of flying yearly on long international flights.

19 . . . to 19 . . .

Pan American Airways, Inc.

New York, NY

Flight Captain. In this position, have had to fly large aircraft; was in complete charge, and in command of crew, craft and passengers during time the plane was in motion. The aircraft that I had to supervise were usually the multimotion type—carrying more than 100 passengers; driven by jet engines or by propellers, running at speeds approaching sound and often flying at higher altitudes because of bad weather. My obligation and supervision started on each flight from the time that I arrived at the airport, usually one or two hours in advance; to do different jobs that had to be done before boarding. Determined such questions as weather possibilities and flight conditions, checking flight plans and obtaining approval from the Federal Aviation Agency air-traffic-control personnel. Once aboard, took part in checking different flight instruments, controls, electronic and mechanical systems.

19 . . . to 19 . . .

United Airlines Corp.

Chicago, IL

Commercial Pilot. By experience and training, was able to meet all the requirements for functioning as a commercial pilot. Piloted airplanes to transport passengers, mail or freight. Reviewed the ship's papers to ascertain such factors as load weight, fuel supply, water conditions, flight route and schedules. Then ordered whatever changes were considered necessary with regard to fuel supply, load, route or schedule to insure safety of flight.

19 . . . to 19 . . .
American Airlines Corp.
New York, NY
Flight Engineer. Assumed this job after obtaining my
regular flight engineer's license from the A.A.A. I
already had my commercial license, which required
indoctrination in the duties expected of a flight
engineer; hence, was assigned to work in several
routes.

EDUCATIONAL BACKGROUND
M.E. Mechanical Engineer, School of Engineering,
Columbia University, New York, NY, 19 . . .
Flying Diploma, Flying School, Mitchell Field, Long
Island City, NY

EARLY BACKGROUND
Grew Up in Brooklyn, NY. Attended public schools in
Brooklyn, NY. Prepared for college at Hamilton High
School, Brooklyn, NY. Member of high school Geo-
graphic Club. Worked summers; employed by
Bayshore Motors, Inc., Long Island City, NY.

PROFESSIONAL MEMBERSHIPS
American Mechanical Society, New York, NY
Airline Pilots Association, Washington, DC
Air Transport Association of America, Washington, DC

OUTSIDE ACTIVITIES
Play tennis, every opportunity offered. Read literature
dealing with my profession, new innovations and
developments. Spend a great deal of time reading
while away from home.

PERSONAL DATA
    Born: 4/5/19 . . .
    Married, 2 children
    Height: 5'10"
    Weight: 165 lbs.
    Yearly physical—meet
        all the requirements
        of F.A.A. flight
        captains.

SALARY
    Open to negotiation, according to duties and respon-
    sibilities, plus complete fringe benefits of the profes-
    sion. (History of salaries available on request.)

REFERENCES
    Character, personal and occupational references
    available on request.

Bank Officer—Modern Analytical Résumé

Thomas F. Bleecker
1 Lafayette Way
Dallas, TX 75230
Date:
Phone: (214)324-5689

SUMMARY OF EXPERIENCE
Familiar with the main routines of a bank in maintaining customer and business relationships, as well as with service and civic organizations, for the purpose of promoting goodwill for the bank and developing and attracting new business. Experienced in supervising personnel that is responsible for accounting and for establishing operating policies and procedures. Have had direct control and custody of assets, records, collateral and securities held by the bank. Familiar with the routine of approving or declining credit for commercial, real-estate and consumer loans.

OCCUPATIONAL OBJECTIVE
To be connected with a bank or similar financial organization in an investment and administrative position where my experience of ten years in banking can be useful, and with potential for promotion according to the development of the activities of the organization.

WORK-RECORD ANALYSIS
19 . . . to present
National Savings Bank
Dallas, TX
Loan-Manager Assistant. Handle installment, commer-

cial, real-estate and other loans. Evaluate loan applications in detail to determine if applicant is eligible and make the final recommendation for granting or denying the loan. In this position, need to be up to date on economic conditions of the community, on distribution and merchandising and/or other regulations as required by law. I possess extensive knowledge of business operations and bank accounting, and know how to analyze financial statements.

19 . . . to 19 . . .
Green Acres Savings Bank
Fort Worth, TX
Trust-Department Assistant. In this position I gained a very extensive and valuable experience in trust management. This field requires a knowledge of financial planning, investments and investment research for person in charge of estates and trust administration. My work produced excellent results as shown by those immediately interested in their investments, and resulted in goodwill for the management of the trust and for the bank.

19 . . . to 19 . . .
The Nelson National Bank
Fort Worth, TX
Administrative-Manager Assistant. In this position, was in charge of Branch 19, where I had to see, plan, coordinate and supervise the work flow, according to latest routines established by the bank, which was striving for administrative efficiency. Required familiarity with general procedures such as electronic data processing in the use and maintenance of information and in the efficient routine functioning of the bank. Had direct supervision over the performance of the duties of each member of the staff in the bank.

EDUCATIONAL BACKGROUND

Dallas University School of Business, New York, NY, *Bachelor of Business Administration*, June 19... Majored in business administration with emphasis on banking, finance and economics. Worked during the summers in a local bank in Dallas.

Took graduate courses in banking and finance in the Dallas University School of Business, Dallas, TX. Also took specialized courses in banking at the American Institute of Banking, Dallas, TX. (19... to 19...)

EARLY BACKGROUND

Grew up in Dallas, TX. Attended public schools; graduated from Johnson High School in 19... Took business courses in typing, accounting, and programming operations.

MILITARY SERVICE

Served in the United States Army for two years, 19... to 19... Attached to the Financial Division of my company.

PROFESSIONAL AFFILIATIONS

American Bankers Association, Dallas, TX
Investment Bankers Association of America, Washington, DC

PROFESSIONAL MEMBERSHIPS

Dallas Chamber of Commerce, Dallas, TX
Texas Youth Rehabilitation Association, Dallas, TX
Health Community Committee, Dallas, TX

PERSONAL INTERESTS

Independent research in financial standing of promising American firms. Swimming, playing tennis, collecting stamps.

PERSONAL DATA
- Born: 19 . . .
- Married, one child
- Health: excellent
- Height: 5'11"
- Weight: 170 lbs.
- Willing to relocate

SALARY

In the $30,000s; open to negotiation according to fringes, locality and potential of the opportunity. (History of salaries available.)

REFERENCES

Professional as well as personal references available.

Bilingual Secretary—
Modern Analytical Résumé

RÉSUMÉ OF
Rose G. Bellins
238 East 68th Street
New York, NY 10021
Date:
Phone: (212)767-3768

SUMMARY OF EXPERIENCE
Complete knowledge and skills in bilingual secretarial work. Able to do translations from English into French and French into English. Complete background of the mechanics of international export and import traffic.

OCCUPATIONAL OBJECTIVE
A connection with a multinational corporation, American or foreign, where my ability as a translator can be utilized to take dictation, and where I can assume management of an international traffic department, as justified by my experience and background.

WORK-RECORD ANALYSIS
19 . . . to 19 . . .
French-American Importers Corp.
New York, NY
French–English Secretary. Was responsible for all secretarial functions and activities such as stenography and correspondence in both languages, telephone traffic, travel arrangements, etc.
    A large part of my major responsibilities was related to import traffic matters such as handling spot sales

contracts, FOB-CIF quotations, export declarations, document receipts and purchases, and sales orders. Had continual telephone contact with brokers in relation to different shipments and documents for import and export transactions. Had to supervise shipper's instructions, letters of destination, debit notes. Kept log of all claims, normal invoices and telexes; maintained delivery and sampling orders; and made additional translations when necessary from French into English and vice versa.

19 . . . to 19 . . .
LaFevre & Jones Corp.
New York, NY
Office-Manager Assistant. Was responsible for all the activities of the busy Bilingual Department, with a minimum of supervision. Handled all the correspondence, received orders from distributors, processed orders through warehouse—duties involving heavy customer-service and phone work. Kept inventory control, ordered merchandise from manufacturers in French. Responsible for all incoming shipments that required close contact with freight forwarders and customs brokers. Acquired a very solid background in international traffic procedures. Represented company at trade shows and was sent to visit factory in France.

EDUCATIONAL BACKGROUND

B.A., Sarah Lawrence College, Bronxville, NY. June 19 . . . Majored in French.

Two summer-school sessions, McGill University, Montreal, Canada.

Specialized in bilingual secretarial course for college graduates, World Trade Academy, New York, NY.

COMMERCIAL SKILLS
Typing, 65 w.p.m. Telex. Stenography, 90 words in English, 80 words in French.

KNOWLEDGE OF LANGUAGES
Fluent knowledge of the French language; working knowledge of Spanish and Italian.

PERSONAL DATA
Born: 19 . . .
Single
Height: 5'6"
Weight: 115 lbs.
Car driver license
Willing to relocate

SALARY
In the $15,000s, open to negotiation. Require all the fringe benefits.

REFERENCES
On request.

_____

Buyer—Modern Analytical Résumé

RÉSUMÉ OF
   Margarete W. Bayerson
   80 Park Ave.
   New York, NY 10016
   Date:
   Tel: (212)687-4598

PERSONAL DATA
   Born: 3/6/19 . . .
   Single
   Height: 5'6"
   Weight: 124 lbs.
   In good health
   Willing to relocate
   Willing to travel

SUMMARY OF EXPERIENCE
   Experienced at purchasing merchandise for resale,
   selecting goods and ordering according to profit possibilities, and attending show rooms of manufacturers
   to examine samples brought in by their representatives and to select products according to kind of
   clientele and the season. Studied accounting reports
   and analyzed the profit or loss in each kind of
   merchandise. Authorized payment of invoices, after
   checking discounts and rechecking quality of goods.
   Selected retail selling prices of new shipments. Supervised and advised selling personnel.

OCCUPATIONAL OBJECTIVE
   To be associated with the buying department of a
   large chain store, department store or national buying
   service.

212

EXPERIENCE HIGHLIGHTS
   19...–19...
   Managing Buyer, R. H. Macy & Co., New York, NY

   19...–19...
   Assistant Buyer in charge of the selection of new
   products, Korvette Stores Corp., New York, NY

EDUCATIONAL RECORD
   Retail Institute, New York University, New York, NY,
   B.S. degree in merchandising, June 19... Majored in
   merchandising, with courses in marketing, buying
   and retailing, and in English, money and banking,
   commercial law, public relations and accounting.
   Financed expenses with money earned in part-time
   employment and summer jobs, plus an allowance
   from my father.

EARLY BACKGROUND
   Grew up in New Hyde Park, NY. Father an engineer
   with Sperry Gyroscope Co. Attended public schools
   and prepared for college at Great Neck High School,
   Great Neck, NY. Graduated *cum laude* with a class of
   approximately 450. Member of the Advertising Club
   and the Home Economics Club.

PROFESSIONAL AFFILIATIONS
   National Association of Purchasing Agents, New York,
   NY
   New York Advertising Club, New York, NY

PERSONAL INTERESTS
   Enjoy extensive reading in technical periodicals in my
   field. Evenings, listen to good music, watch the better
   television shows. During the summer, enjoy swimming and tennis.

SALARY

In the $25,000s. (History of salaries on request.)

REFERENCES

References available on request.

Chemical Engineer—
Modern Analytical Résumé

RÉSUMÉ OF
   William M. Bowker
   180 Orange Road
   Montclair, NJ 07042
   Date: 19 . . .
   Telephone: (201)717-4391

SUMMARY OF EXPERIENCE
   Involved in all activities concerned with chemical
   engineering. Am competent to plan, design and take
   an active part in the construction of chemical plants or
   in the installation of additional equipment. Have been
   very active in research with a view to developing new
   and improved processes for production resulting in
   greater financial benefits to my employers.

OCCUPATIONAL OBJECTIVE
   To be placed in the capacity of chief chemical engineer
   responsible for product development and technical
   research on new applications.

EXPERIENCE HIGHLIGHTS
   19 . . . to present
   Allied Chemical Corp.
   Morristown, NJ
   This firm is a major manufacturer of starch, resins and
   adhesives. It employs about 2,000 people and grosses
   about $100,000,000 yearly.

Product-Development Engineer. Assigned as product-development chemical engineer in company laboratory and plant. Responsible for modifications and research in the development of resins, i.e., vinyl acetate, vinyl chloride acrylate, thermosetting, polyesters, epoxy.

Develop products for paper, textile, paint, protective-coating and related industries. Also assigned as technical service representative responsible for training chemists and salesmen on product line and supporting activities of seven sales representatives. Work directly with national firms located east of Mississippi.

19 . . . to 19 . . .
Eli Lilly Company
Indianapolis, IN
This company does research and development in the manufacture and sale of chemical fibers, electronics materials and instruments. Average number of employees, 60,000. Average yearly sales, $1 billion to $2 billion.

Chemical Engineer. Conducted research to develop new and improved chemically manufactured products. Designed research program and was overseer of workers engaged in the construction, control and improvement of equipment for carrying out chemical processes for the production of better products. Determined most effective arrangement of operations such as mixing, crushing, heat transfer, distillation, oxidation, hydrogenation and polymerization. Supervised workers controlling equipment such as condensers in absorption and evaporation towers, columns and stills.

EDUCATION
The Polytechnic Institute of Brooklyn, Brooklyn, NY.

M.S. in Polymer Chemistry, June 19 . . . Followed regular curriculum. In addition to the required courses in chemistry, also took social sciences, contemporary civilization, industrial production of United States. Made the Dean's List. Member of Tau Epsilon Sigma (scholastic honor society). Elected to Delta Kappa Phi fraternity (social). Member of the editorial board of *Pickout*, the school yearbook.

MILITARY SERVICE

U. S. Army. Volunteered for six months of active duty. Reserve obligation completed as of July 19 . . .

PROFESSIONAL AFFILIATIONS

Chemical Engineering Society, New York, NY
American Chemical Society, Washington, DC

EARLY BACKGROUND

Grew up in New York City. Son of a physician who has his own practice and is professor of internal medicine at the College of Physicians and Surgeons, Columbia University, New York, NY. Attended New York City public schools and prepared for college at Dwight School for Boys. Graduated *cum laude*. Elected president of senior class of 120 boys. Member of the Mathematics Club and Science Club. Played intramural football and tennis.

PERSONAL INTERESTS

Read and play golf as time permits.

OUTSIDE ACTIVITIES

Active in community and local politics.

PERSONAL DATA

Born: 6/22/19 . . .,
Worcester, MA

Single
Health: excellent
Height: 6 ft.
Weight: 175 lbs.

SALARY

Open to negotiation in the $25,000s. (History of salaries available.)

REFERENCES

Available on request.

College Instructor—
Modern Analytical Résumé

RÉSUMÉ OF
Charles B. Burns
1030 N. Dearborn
Chicago, IL 60610
Date:
Phone: (312)792-6348

SUMMARY OF EXPERIENCE

I have served as an instructor and professor, teaching different courses in the field of economics. Besides lecturing, have done some research to supplement my income. I have written articles on economic questions for several professional magazines and newspapers. Have taught between 8 and 12 hours weekly, spending time in preparation for my classes and in the correction of papers and final grading at the end of each semester. My methods of teaching have been a combination of lecturing plus analysis of cases.

OCCUPATIONAL OBJECTIVE

To serve on the faculty of a well-established economics department of a large university, or as a research economist for a private financial organization in the fields of marketing or international direct investments.

EXPERIENCE HIGHLIGHTS
19 . . . to 19 . . .
School of Business, Northwestern University
Chicago, IL
Assistant Professor of Business Administration. The courses that I taught at Northwestern included

money and banking, current economic problems, management and administration. These are highly specialized and were taken mostly by seniors or students working for their master's degree. Have supervised the preparation of master's theses, and also have done a great deal of research in the fields of banking, money and distribution of wealth for the National Bank & Trust Co. of Chicago, IL.

19 . . . to 19 . . .
DePaul University
Chicago, IL

Instructor in Economic Analysis. Besides teaching, I also engaged in research for the university, which accepts research studies on money matters, production and labor problems for the federal government, labor unions, banks or financial organizations. Such projects are financed in order to obtain answers that can be used as tools for the promotion and expansion of their activities. The teaching load was not very heavy, but the courses were quite advanced: corporate management, marketing analysis of specialized consumer products, and other courses of a similar nature.

19 . . . to 19 . . .
Roosevelt University
Chicago, IL

Instructor in Economics. The teaching schedule in this college was quite heavy, because it required a great deal of preparation for my lectures and the correction of papers assigned to the students. Taught several sections of Economics I and Economics II, which covered the basic principles of the subject. Using Leon Eddie's *Principles of Economics* as a textbook gave the student an excellent analytical background and a solid basis for understanding the economic structure of society.

EDUCATION

19 . . . to 19 . . .

University of Chicago, Chicago, IL.

Master of Business Administration Degree, June 19 . . .
Studied general program for broad diversification
of economics and economic-research background.
Elective courses in advanced production problems,
money and central banking, national income and
employment, public finance. Thesis: "Money and
Direct Investments in Foreign Countries."

19 . . . to 19 . . .

University of Chicago, Chicago, IL.

A.B. Degree, June 19 . . . Majored in economics. Other
courses: English, social sciences, industrial organization, public policy. President of Delta Kappa
Epsilon fraternity. Member of the debating team.
Played intramural tennis. Worked in bank part-
time.

LITERARY ACCOMPLISHMENTS

*Books: Money and Direct Investments in Foreign Coun-
tries,* World Trade Press, Inc., 19 . . .

Articles: "A Comprehensive Survey of Foreign Direct
Investments in the United States," *Money
Matters,* June, 19 . . .

"Study of the Management Practices of the
100 Leading Corporations in the United
States," *American Management,* September,
19 . . .

EARLY BACKGROUND

Grew up in Chicago, IL. Father a professor of business
administration at the University of Southern Illinois,
Carbondale, IL. Attended public schools in Highland

Park, IL, and Evanston High School. Spent most summers during school and college years working for the Continental Bank in Chicago.

PROFESSIONAL MEMBERSHIPS
American Marketing Society, Chicago, IL
Rotary International Club of Chicago, Chicago, IL

PERSONAL INTERESTS
Enjoy golf, tennis and swimming. Write a great deal during the academic year and during the summer.

FINANCES
Finances in good condition. Own real estate in Highland Park, IL. Own condominium apartment. Own two cars. Carry a good insurance policy.

PERSONAL DATA
Born: 6/14/19...
Married, 2 children
Height: 5'10"
Weight: 165 lbs.
Wear glasses
Good health, yearly
   physical

SALARY
In the $30,000s plus benefits. (History of salaries and other earnings through research available.)

REFERENCES
Excellent character and professional references available.

Commercial Translator—Modern
Analytical Résumé

RÉSUMÉ OF

George H. Mahar
350 Market St.
San Francisco, CA
94110
Date:
Phone: (415)789-3654

SUMMARY OF EXPERIENCE

Am an experienced free-lance translator. Have handled correspondence for large foreign departments of multinational corporations with more than 20 subsidiaries in Europe and Latin America. Know how to prepare material for promotion in foreign countries using local idiom. Can translate legal material that is of importance to firms that have branches, subsidiaries or licensees in countries where Spanish, Portuguese, or French is the language used.

OCCUPATIONAL OBJECTIVE

Looking for employment with a company that, through its international commercial relations, requires a competent translator from Spanish, Portuguese, French, Italian or German into English, and from English into these foreign languages. Have had considerable experience in commercial correspondence, export and import documentation, and preparation and translation of promotional material as well as of technical guides and legal contracts.

19 . . .–19 . . .

Bechtel Corp.

San Francisco, CA

Commercial Translator. Though my title was "commercial translator," there were other important duties that I performed in this office. Among these duties were devising technical papers and blueprints connected with construction projects in foreign countries, and making translations from Spanish to English and English to Spanish. If a language that I could not translate was required, it was my responsibility to locate a free-lance translator who could do the work. These translations were under the supervision of the legal department of the company.

19 . . .–19 . . .

Thomas Marketing and Development Co.

San Jose, CA

Commercial Translator. In this position I was in charge of receiving and reading all foreign correspondence, which I had to translate into English for the attention of those executives who handled the matters referred to. Once the problem or question in the correspondence was answered, it was my task to dictate the answer. Most of the correspondence from abroad was in French, Spanish or German. I had the help of three bilingual secretaries in this work.

EDUCATIONAL BACKGROUND

B.A. in Communications, June 19 . . . from University of California, Berkeley, CA. Majored in Romance languages, where my French background was very important as a basis for studying other languages.

MILITARY SERVICE

U.S. Army, four years of active duty in Europe. The title of my job was translator-interpreter (04B).

224

MEMBERSHIPS
  The U.S. Chamber of Commerce, Washington, DC
  Latin American Chambers of Commerce, New York,
    NY

PERSONAL AFFILIATIONS
  World Trade Club, San Francisco, CA
  European Chamber of Commerce, San Francisco, CA

PERSONAL DATA
  Born: 8/7/19 . . .
  Married, one child
  Height: 6'0"
  Weight: 185 lbs.
  Good health
  Willing to relocate, if
    position merits

SALARY
  In the $20,000s plus fringe benefits, and possibilities
  of promotion and accomplishment in the field of
  international marketing. History of salaries available.

REFERENCES
  Character and personal information on request.

RÉSUMÉ OF

John Jay Bliss
318 Epic Road
Richmond, VA 23235
Date:
Phone: (804)987-3255

SUMMARY OF EXPERIENCE

Am familiar with and experienced in establishing
office procedures relating to credits and collections.
Can supervise workers who gather information,
analyze facts and perform general office duties in the
credit department. Am efficient in analyzing the facts
for granting credit, and when to press for the collection
of moneys due.

OCCUPATIONAL OBJECTIVE

To secure a position as credits and collections manager
with a firm that can use the services of an experienced
man—a firm that offers possibilities for advancement
and expresses appreciation through financial rewards.

WORK-RECORD ANALYSIS

19 . . . to 19 . . .
Richmond Mercantile Credit Corp.
Richmond, VA
Credit Manager. In this position I had daily supervision
of the analysis of credit requests. Have had the
authority to make the final decision whether to
accept or to reject a credit application. Credit peti-

tions were mostly from businesses and individuals who needed credit to meet their business needs.

19 . . . to 19 . . .
Wilson, Walker Associates, Inc.
Roanoke, VA
Assistant Credit and Collections Manager. In this position, was responsible for gathering all information necessary to granting the credit asked for by small manufacturers in nearby communities. Analyzed detailed reports submitted by the applicant, and interviewed said applicant when necessary. Represented the company as part of its management, established why the credit was wanted and made a final report approving or rejecting the ability of the applicant to repay the debt.

19 . . . to 19 . . .
Hellenic Manufacturing Co.
Richmond, VA
Sales-Department Credit Manager. Secured a position with this furniture manufacturer after graduation from college. Cooperated with the sales force in developing a credit policy that would increase business and yet be strict enough to deny credit to customers whose ability to repay their debts was doubtful.

EDUCATIONAL BACKGROUND
Richmond University, Richmond, VA. *B.S. Degree in Business Administration*, June 19 . . . The courses provided a sound grasp of the tools of analysis and measurement and an understanding of institutional development and interrelations in our business society. Am able to apply systematic analysis to economic and business problems. College expenses financed mainly through family allowance.

EARLY BACKGROUND

Grew up in Richmond, VA. Father executive of the Reynolds Tobacco Co. Attended public schools in Richmond and prepared for college at Robert E. Lee High School at Richmond, VA. Member of the intramural football team for the last three years. Most summers during high school and college years spent at family's place at Martinsville, VA.

PERSONAL INTERESTS

Golf, swimming, tennis; reading technical literature and current events

PERSONAL DATA

Born: 3/17/19 . . .
Married, 2 children
Church affiliation, active
   member of Our
   Redeemer Lutheran
   Church
Height: 6'9"
Weight: 175 lbs.
Excellent health
Will relocate

SALARY

In the $25,000s plus fringe benefits. (History of salaries available.)

REFERENCES

Personal and business references available on request.

228

Design Engineer—
Modern Analytical Résumé

RÉSUMÉ OF

Herbert Sussman
515 Boston Pl.
Buffalo, NY 14216
Date:
Phone: (716)785-9543

SUMMARY OF EXPERIENCE

Can offer more than seven years of experience and related educational background in the field of engineering design. All my positions have required imaginative designing for a wide range of products and equipment. Functioned as operations engineer in designing and construction of petroleum oil blending and distribution plants, and in their instrumentation. Have performed the functions of service manager and technical advisor for large-tonnage centrifugal and absorption chillers.

OCCUPATIONAL OBJECTIVE

Looking for a position that offers an excellent salary and benefits, along with outstanding prospects for promotion and advancement.

HIGHLIGHTS OF EXPERIENCE

19...–19...
Cool Air Manufacturing Corp.
Buffalo, NY
Design Engineer. This company is a specialized and important operating unit of a large national corporation where my work was mostly with centrifugal

pumps and steam or gas turbines. Was responsible for the design, development and application of boiler feed pumps. Here I had to show a broad-based capability, as distinct from dealing with only component parts. My work gave me factory exposure to assembling and testing the finished product. It was challenging and demanding work, and gave me the opportunity to design and redesign this type of equipment.

19 . . . –19 . . .
H.K. Construction Equipment Co.
Schenectady, NY
Structural-Design Engineer. This company specializes in making construction equipment, cement-manufacturing equipment. I was responsible for the design of industrial-plant-type structures. The work included the design of heavy-machinery foundations, concrete or steel storage silos, general plant engineering. I needed to be thoroughly familiar with current concrete and steel codes, including soils engineering, and know how to handle heavy mechanical equipment. Worked independently on a wide variety of problems in connection with designing cement plants.

EDUCATIONAL BACKGROUND
B.M.E. (Bachelor of Mechanical Engineering), June 19 . . ., Rensselaer Polytechnic Institute, Troy, NY. For design and manufacturing processes, took such courses as engineering drawing, metallurgy, machine design, industrial engineering and manufacturing engineering. Financed my education through scholarship, allowance from home and part-time work in drafting and designing.

230

EARLY BACKGROUND

Grew up in New York City. Son of mechanical engineer with Union Carbon and Carbide, New York, NY. Attended public schools, prepared for college at De-Witt Clinton High School, New York, NY; graduated 19 . . . Played intramural football. Member of the Science Club.

PROFESSIONAL MEMBERSHIPS

American Society of Mechanical Engineers, New York, NY

Industrial Society of Designers of America, McLean, VA

LICENSE

Professional Engineer, New York, NY

PERSONAL INTERESTS

Enjoy swimming and tennis.
Interested in creating new mechanical devices.

PERSONAL DATA

Born: 9/10/19 . . .,
   White Plains, NY
Married, 2 children
Good health
Height: 5'11"
Weight: 170 lbs.
Willing to relocate
   within United States

SALARY

In the $35,000s, plus benefits and advancement guaranty. History of salaries available.

REFERENCES

Available on request.

Executive Secretary—
Modern Analytical Résumé

RÉSUMÉ OF
Esther H. Hilton
3422 29th St., N.W.
Washington, DC 20008
Date:
Phone: (202)567-4576

SUMMARY OF EXPERIENCE

Can take and transcribe dictation, and prepare reports on directives and telephone conversations for which a record is desired. Can record proceedings of conferences, staff meetings and committees, using shorthand or a shorthand machine. Can handle correspondence and perform related administrative duties on my own initiative.

OBJECTIVE

To secure a position in private industry or with a national organization whose headquarters are in Washington, DC, and where I can demonstrate my administrative and executive ability. Am changing jobs at this time because my current connection is closing its Washington office.

EXPERIENCE RECORD

19 . . .–19 . . .

Industrial Research & Development Corp.

Washington, DC

Administrative Secretary. Apart from the secretarial functions in this position, my duties were mostly concentrated on performing some of my employer's

232

administrative tasks so that he could devote his time to more important matters.

19...–19...
National Association of Manufacturers
Washington, DC
Executive Secretary. In this position I served as executive secretary to one of the executives in charge of developing the activities of the National Association of Manufacturers. In addition to my regular secretarial duties, was responsible for taking care of desk matters during my employer's absence from town. This happened quite often. I handled a great deal of correspondence, did statistical research and wrote press releases regarding meetings. Left for a better salary.

19...–19...
Rockwell International, Inc.
New York, NY
Secretary. My duties with this firm included answering general correspondence, taking dictation on important matters and receiving callers. I left this position because the company relocated elsewhere.

EDUCATION

Katherine Gibbs Secretarial School graduate of a two-year secretarial course, where I learned how to write and answer letters and manage an office. Through the school I obtained my first job with Rockwell International.

EARLY BACKGROUND

Grew up in Smithtown, L.I., NY. Father a corporation lawyer for Edison Corporation. Attended schools in Smithtown, NY. Graduated from Long Beach High School. Member of the Home Economics Club.

PERSONAL INTERESTS
Theatre, music, tennis and swimming

MEMBERSHIP
National Secretaries Association, Kansas City, MO

PERSONAL DATA
Born: 5/18/19...
Single
Height: 5'5"
Weight: 120 lbs.
Excellent health
Willing to relocate, if
   position merits

SALARY
In the $15,000s, open to negotiation in accordance
with benefits, location of job and duties.

REFERENCES
Excellent references on request.

234

Foreign-Marketing Manager—Modern Analytical Résumé

RÉSUMÉ OF
Gary Feldman
312 West Huron
Chicago, IL 60618
Date:
Phone: (312)897-6782

SUMMARY OF EXPERIENCE

Have had ten years of experience as a marketing executive, conducting research, planning, promoting and developing programs that led to company expansion and strengthened financial position. Possess the necessary background in domestic and international marketing and sales promotion.

OBJECTIVE

To be associated with the Marketing Department of a multinational corporation, where proven ability and successful performance can be utilized to mutual advantage.

HIGHLIGHTS OF EXPERIENCE

19...–19...
Robinson Manufacturing Co.
Skokie, IL

International-Marketing Manager. Surveyed international market areas to determine potential sales of the products of the company. Major duties included obtaining market data on existing services, establishing and maintaining market data base, conducting research on new services, providing analysis for market-planning purposes, compiling data on competitors for analysis, and providing assistance to field sales staff and to special-project efforts in foreign-field areas.

19...–19...
Allyson Equipment, Inc.
Chicago, IL
Market-Research Manager. This position provided the opportunity to make decisions at every functional level relating to products. Reported to the Marketing Division Vice-President. Assumed total product management and responsibility for our motion-compensation equipment line. Became aware of and intimately involved in every product aspect, from research and development concepts to manufacturing, marketing, pricing, and sales and service through customer relations.

EDUCATION
University of Michigan, Ann Arbor, MI. *M.B.A. Degree,* February 19 . . . Majored in marketing, with emphasis on analysis of business problems and understanding managerial principles as they related to case studies in market research, industrial marketing and advertising.

University of Michigan. *B.B.A. Degree,* February 19 . . . Concentrated on building a strong foundation in all fields of business, including accounting, finance, economics, statistics and management. Member of Delta Tau Delta.

EARLY BACKGROUND
Raised in Oak Park, IL. Father employed by tire and rubber company. Mother a schoolteacher. Graduated from Oak Park High School, Oak Park, IL.

KNOWLEDGE OF FOREIGN LANGUAGES
    Spanish: read, write and speak fluently

PROFESSIONAL MEMBERSHIPS
    American Marketing Association, Chicago, IL
    Foreign Trade Council, Inc., New York, NY
    Chicago Export Club, Chicago, IL

PERSONAL INTERESTS
    Fishing, sports cars and photography when time permits

PERSONAL DATA
    Born: 8/15/19...
    Married, one child
    Height: 5'8"
    Weight: 155 lbs.

SALARY
    In the $30,000s plus benefits. History of salaries available.

REFERENCES
    Available on request.

Industrial Engineer—
Modern Analytical Résumé

RÉSUMÉ OF
Edward N. Myers
1030 N. Dearborn
Chicago, IL 60602
Date:
Phone: (303)277-3756

OBJECTIVE

Position in metal-work industry as chief industrial engineer, where the experience and training of the past 18 years can be used for the benefit of the company, and where there is an opportunity of increasing responsibility on top management level.

EXPERIENCE RECORD

Chief Industrial Engineer. Harrison, Inc., Chicago, IL, 19 . . . to present.

This firm manufactures razors, blades and electric shavers, and small metal components of a precision nature. It employs approximately 1,800 people and grosses about $40,000,000 a year. I started with this company as supervisor of time study with four engineers under me. Having established a program of setting time studies, I had completely covered every job in the plant within eight months. One year later I was placed in charge of the entire Industrial Engineering Division as chief industrial engineer, where I supervised a staff of 25 engineers, methods men and time-study men, and had full charge of all industrial-engineering activities.

Installed a job-evaluation plant (point-factor) and received the enthusiastic cooperation of the union.

Improved manufacturing methods, which resulted in a cost reduction of over 35 percent on one product alone. Installed a system of tool-inventory control that, by means of proper systematizing of records, reduced tool losses by 21 percent. Prepared special cost analysis of products by operation and pointed out products that should be dropped because of lack of volume, too high production costs and excessive tooling charges. Acted as management representative in several contract negotiations.

Industrial Engineer. Baker Machine Co., Chicago, IL, 19...–19...

This is a small lock company, manufacturing special locks for industrial purposes. It employs approximately 175 people and grosses about $6,000,000 yearly. In this capacity, I supervised several assistants and five junior engineers. Had complete responsibility for the establishment of labor standards in the manufacturing and foundry operations. Had charge of all timekeeping, and of administration of the job-evaluation plan (installed by outside consultants). Acted as management representative in dealing with the union. Developed and installed production-control system.

Staff Engineer. Meridian, Inc., Ft. Wayne, IN, 19...–19...

This is a well-known firm of management consultants. As staff engineer, I participated in manufacturing-facilities surveys and top-management organization surveys. Participated in the survey and installation of a manufacturing-cost control plan and of a Labor-Cost Determination for installation of standard costs. Worked on problems in the airplane, drug, dye and textile fields.

Supervisor of Planning and Wage Rates. Robinson Electric Co., Chicago, IL, 19 . . .–19 . . .

I started with this large electrical manufacturing company as a time-study man and within one year was made chief timekeeper, subsequently serving as methods man, job analyst, supervisor of wage rates, and finally as supervisor of planning and wage rates, in which capacity I planned and laid out a $10,000,000 special new project.

EDUCATION

B.S. in industrial engineering, University of Michigan, Milwaukee, WI, 19 . . .

PROFESSIONAL AFFILIATIONS

American Management Association
American Society of Industrial Engineers
Society for the Advancement of Management

PERSONAL DATA

Age 41—Married, 2
children
Excellent health
Height: 6'1"
Weight: 200 lbs.

SALARY

Salary in the $35,000s. (List of salaries on request.)

REFERENCES

On request.

Industrial-Traffic Manager—Modern Analytical Résumé

RÉSUMÉ OF

Edward B. Kleinberg
17 Morris Street
New York, NY 10006
Date:
Phone: (212)567-4531

SUMMARY OF EXPERIENCE

As an industrial-traffic manager I am able to analyze and choose the most convenient possibilities—rail, air, road, water or some combination of these—for transporting merchandise. I always did the selecting of the route and the carrier, and in doing this I had to consider such factors as freight classifications and the applicable regulations. I have a complete record of experience in the industrial-traffic field.

OCCUPATIONAL OBJECTIVE

To be connected with a large manufacturing company in the Middle West or on the West Coast. Because of illness in the family I need to relocate in these areas.

WORK-RECORD ANALYSIS

19 . . . to 19 . . .
Mercury Manufacturing Co.
Northvale, NJ

Industrial-Traffic Manager. The above is a very large chemicals-pharmaceuticals manufacturer, with a sales total of over $500 million yearly. The company is very active in marketing and merchandising its products. The traffic manager has the very responsible function of securing and arranging the best method of transporting the company's products. He exercises his judgment in relation to the final destination and considers such factors as the distance to be covered and regulations regarding interstate transportation and shipment to foreign countries.

19 . . . to 19 . . .
Watson Manufacturing Co.
Summit, NJ

Traffic Manager. In this position I had to study and become familiar with the vehicular-traffic conditions in urban and rural routes. I also had to consider changing conditions and develop plans to deal with them for safety. No small part of my job was to analyze traffic conditions as they related to the warehouse, and the vehicle of transport, in order to detect possible delays or unsafe routes.

19 . . . to 19 . . .
Minerals and Chemical Corp.
Newark, NJ

Traffic Manager. In this job I routed and traced shipments, arranged with carriers for transportation services, prepared bills of lading and other shipping documents, and handled claims for lost or damaged goods. Worked closely with production executives to plan shipping schedules, and with members of the purchasing department to evaluate the most economical ways of transporting goods in different quantities.

EDUCATIONAL BACKGROUND

B.S. in commerce and business administration, Baruch College, University of the City of New York, New York, NY. Majored in transportation.

EARLY BACKGROUND

Grew up in Teaneck, NJ. Father an executive of Stern Department Store, Paramus, NJ. Attended Teaneck High School. Member of intramural football team, junior and senior years. Traveled in Europe and South America during summers, working for different steamship companies.

PROFESSIONAL AFFILIATIONS

American Marketing Association, Chicago, IL
American Society of Traffic and Transportation, Inc., Chicago, IL

PERSONAL INTERESTS

Very active during last 8 years in the annual Red Cross drive. Take active part in community affairs. Swimming and tennis as time permits.

PERSONAL DATA

Age: 36
Married, 2 daughters
Excellent health
Last physical, 19 . . .
Height: 5'9"
Weight: 160 lbs.
Willing to relocate

SALARY

In the $20,000s plus good fringe benefits. History of salaries available on request.

REFERENCES

Personal and business references available on request.

International-Marketing Analyst—Modern Analytical Résumé

RÉSUMÉ OF

Olivia D. Rasmusen
1301 Fillmore Avenue
Chicago, IL 60607
Date:
Phone: (312)243-5271

SUMMARY OF EXPERIENCE

Have handled international-marketing research problems through collecting, analyzing and interpreting data relative to existing markets and new territory being considered. Estimated potential of a product or service. Prepared reports and made recommendations on subjects ranging from preferences of prospective customers to methods and costs of distribution and advertising. I designed methods of distribution and sale deduced from printed matter and the accumulation of new data through personal interviews and questionnaires, when the volume demanded this specialized approach.

OCCUPATIONAL OBJECTIVE

To be connected with a firm or organization that specializes in international marketing, and that needs or can use an experienced officer in the development of international-marketing projects for the company or for customers of the firm.

EXPERIENCE HIGHLIGHTS

19 . . . to 19 . . .
Williamson Manufacturing Co.
Skokie, IL

244

Market-Analyst Director. Served as a consultant and reorganizer. I was able in numerous instances to save the management from repeating past mistakes—such as increasing prices in a declining market, promoting new products in the face of buying reluctance, utilizing the wrong advertising or sales approaches.

19 . . . to 19 . . .
Eagle Appliances Manufacturing Co.
Chicago, IL
International-Market Analyst. My experience in this position covered everything from consumer research to policy and planning, advertising and sales promotion. My work and decisions, as well as the organization of the research, contributed a great deal to the economic strengthening of the company and the steady increase in its annual profits.

19 . . . to 19 . . .
Housewares Appliances Manufacturing Company
Rockford, IL
Procedures-Analyst Officer. Prepared and conducted programs to analyze different types of selling campaigns. Hired and trained my staff for research and analysis of the project in hand, or for several projects at the same time. My programs stimulated and increased international sales by introducing new products overseas. Reduced the advertising budget. Determined consumer buying trends, which permitted correct forecasting.

EDUCATIONAL BACKGROUND
B.S. in marketing, 19 . . ., Roosevelt University, Chicago, IL

EARLY BACKGROUND

Grew up in Evanston, IL. Father Supermarket Manager in Evanston, IL. Graduated from Evanston High School. Member of the Mathematics Club. Worked as cashier in supermarket during the summer months.

PROFESSIONAL AFFILIATIONS

Member of the National Foreign Trade Council, New York, NY
American Marketing Association, Chicago, IL
Member of the Export Club, Chicago, IL

PERSONAL INTERESTS

Playing tennis and attending adult classes in the field of International Commercial Relations at Northwestern University, Chicago, IL.

PERSONAL DATA

Born: 6/3/19 . . .
Married
Height: 5'7"
Weight: 130 lbs.
Good health
Willing to travel 25% of
the time

SALARY

In the $25,000s, plus fringe benefits. History of salaries available.

REFERENCES

Good references on request.

Junior Copywriter—
Modern Analytical Résumé

RÉSUMÉ OF
Paula M. Decker
77 Park Ave.
New York, NY 10016
Date:
Phone: (212)789-5672

SUMMARY OF EXPERIENCE

Some products are made to appeal and be sold to special groups, such as housewives, businessmen or professionals. These products are advertised through such media as radio, television, newspapers, billboards. I have gained considerable experience as a copywriter in preparing copy for the different media as mentioned. I am particularly well qualified to prepare copy for those with special interests: physicians, paramedical workers, technicians and white collar personnel. I have a practical background in working with the copy chief or the advertising account executive in an organization.

OBJECTIVE

To be employed with a well-established advertising agency that is doing over $75 million a year in business, and where my creative ability and effective writing skill can be put to full use. Another one of my objectives is a job in which the possibilities for promotion are not limited to copywriting alone, but one that will also offer opportunity for growth in the executive and administrative aspects of advertising, and compensation in accordance with growth.

19 . . . to present
Murray Hill Advertising Co.
New York, NY

Junior Advertising Copywriter. In this job I am required
to do a great deal of research in connection with the
product to be advertised. The research includes
gathering information about the consumer who will
use the product. After completing the research as
indicated, I write descriptive copy that will result in
more people buying the product advertised.

19 . . .–19 . . .

Wilson Bros. Advertising Co.
New York, NY

Junior Copywriter Assistant. My duties here were to
write copy about the product advertised, using the
ideas submitted to me by the account executive. The
writing of copy included such specialties as devising
jingles, making up slogans and thinking up other
means of attracting potential buyers. I also wrote
copy for automobiles; television equipment, electric
appliances and similar products.

19 . . .–19 . . .
Marx, Wrigley Advertising Co.
New York, NY

Copywriter Assistant Manager. Here I created and wrote
final copy, slogans and text to attract and increase
sales among the consumer public. I had to study
carefully all the information submitted to me by the
promotion manager of the manufacturer, as well as
the best consumer markets for the product. Using my
copywriting background together with my
psychological insights, I was able to prepare excellent copy that brought financial results.

EDUCATIONAL BACKGROUND

Pace University, New York, NY, B.S. Degree in business administration, June 19 . . . Majored in advertising. Courses included marketing, business finance, business management and marketing research, as well as several specialized courses in English by means of which I developed my ability to write effective copy. All college expenses paid by family and part-time earnings while working for the *New York Day.*

EARLY BACKGROUND

Grew up in Haddonfield, NJ. Educated in public schools, prepared for college at Haddonfield High School, Haddonfield, NJ. Member of the Writers Club. Traveled through Europe and South America during summers, as companion to a lady in our community.

PERSONAL INTERESTS

Enjoy golf, tennis and swimming, as time permits. Keen interest in community activities.

OUTSIDE ACTIVITIES

Member of a political club in my neighborhood.

PROFESSIONAL MEMBERSHIPS

Advertising Federation of America (AFA), New York, NY
International Advertising Association, New York, NY

PERSONAL BACKGROUND

Born: 6/21/19 . . .
Single
Height: 5'7"
Weight: 125 lbs.
Excellent health

Will relocate, if
opportunity merits

SALARY

In the $20,000s, open to negotiation if opportunity merits. History of salaries available.

REFERENCES

Character and professional references available on request.

_____

Manufacturer's Salesman—Modern Analytical Résumé

RÉSUMÉ OF
Oliver G. Green
315 Sullivan W.
Chicago, IL 60610
Date:
Phone: (312)568-7890

SUMMARY OF EXPERIENCE
Have technical experience as a successful manufacturer's salesman, representing several companies that sell machinery and machinery parts and utilizing knowledge of operating such machinery and of how it is put together. Can compute cost of installing machinery and possible savings in production costs through such installation.

OCCUPATIONAL OBJECTIVE
To be able to work with large machinery manufacturer as sales engineer where, besides understanding the functions of the equipment, I can work with the research and development department, devising ways to adapt products to a customer's specialized needs.

HIGHLIGHTS OF EXPERIENCE
19 . . . to 19 . . .
Sales Engineer. Manufacturers International Corp., Summit, NJ. In this position I have had to deal with highly technical equipment and parts. Since I had complete understanding and knowledge of the firm's products, I was able to help prospective

251

buyers with technical problems in the use of equipment and in determining the proper materials to be used in the manufacturing process.

19 . . . to 19 . . .

Industrial Salesman. J. Albertson Equipment Machinery Co., Riverside, IL. In this position, called at industrial and commercial establishments. Also called on engineers, architects and other professional and technical workers, attempting to convince prospective customers of the importance of purchasing from my company. Usually had to prepare financial and operational estimates from blueprints, plans or other records submitted by the potential customer.

19 . . . to 19 . . .

Manufacturer's Salesman. Power Machinery & Equipment Corp., Elk Grove Village, IL. This work demanded wide-ranging involvement that included supervising proposed development, assuring compatibility with regional business customs and participating in the sales presentation of power plants. Was responsible for developing home-office supportive sources, and for coordinating activities in support of the area sales representatives.

EDUCATIONAL BACKGROUND

19 . . . to 19 . . .

B.S. Degree in Mechanical Engineering. Stevens Institute of Technology, Union City, NJ. Followed the institute's regular curriculum for this degree. Played intramural football. Expenses financed mainly through family allowance.

PROFESSIONAL AFFILIATION

American Mechanical Engineers Society, New York, NY

EARLY BACKGROUND

Grew up in West New York, NJ. Father manager of supermarket in Hoboken. Educated in public schools and prepared for college at West New York High School. During the summers helped my father in the accounting department.

OUTSIDE ACTIVITIES

Attending graduate courses connected with my profession in mechanical-equipment development.

PERSONAL ACTIVITIES

Enjoy sailing, fishing. As I am greatly interested in community affairs, have worked, while in Chicago, under a social-service program at Hull House.

PERSONAL DATA

Age: 40
Married
Height: 5'9"
Weight: 155 lbs.
Good health

SALARY

In the $30,000s plus commission and fringe benefits. (History of salaries available.)

REFERENCES

Character and professional, available on request.

Manuscript Editor—
Modern Analytical Résumé

RÉSUMÉ OF
   Janet L. Brown
   80 Park Avenue
   New York, NY 10016
   Date:
   Phone: (212)655-3647

SUMMARY OF EXPERIENCE

Experienced in reading and evaluating manuscripts for books and magazine articles. Able to determine and advise as to the acceptance or rejection of a manuscript. When in charge of an editorial job, can improve the material by evaluating and rewriting it. Possess the background for determining public acceptance of the book or article.

OCCUPATIONAL OBJECTIVE

My present position offers no further challenge and I want a connection with a publisher where my experience in the editorial field can be of mutual benefit— where I can do final editorial work, and be allowed to offer an opinion as to the value of a manuscript, its advantages and disadvantages, and possible public reaction if published.

EXPERIENCE HIGHLIGHTS
   19 . . . to 19 . . .
   Park Book Corp.
   New York, NY
   Book-Editor Assistant. Improved manuscripts for publication. Prepared books, along with their designs,

layouts and photographic materials, prior to having them sent to the printer.

19 . . . to 19 . . .
Hearst Publications, Inc.
New York, NY

Manuscript Editor and Rewriter. Collected material for feature articles through personal interviews, library research and transcribing events. Wrote picture captions and headlines. Assisted in the production of the magazine.

19 . . . to 19 . . .
Fortune Magazine
New York, NY

Assistant in the Editorial Department. Worked in the editorial department as an editorial assistant. Took active part in the research of the more important articles that required a great deal of information and preparation. Also helped in putting together first drafts and in the improvement of style and contents, as assigned by supervisor.

EDUCATIONAL BACKGROUND
19 . . . to 19 . . .

Bachelor of Arts Degree, Sarah Lawrence College, Brownsville, NY. June 19 . . . Majored in English with courses in writing, sociology, philosophy, history, economics and government. Three years as news and managing editor of *Sarah Lawrence News;* duties included writing editorials, handling administrative details and developing original ideas. Member of Public Relations and Publicity Club.

EARLY BACKGROUND
Grew up in Yonkers, NY. Attended public schools; was

graduated from Yonkers High School, June 19...
Took special courses in shorthand and typing.

PROFESSIONAL MEMBERSHIP

Association of Magazine Writers, New York, NY

OUTSIDE ACTIVITIES

Take active part in professional organizations such as
American Editors Society, National Rehabilitation
Club, and Foster Parents Plan.

PERSONAL INTERESTS

Enjoy swimming and dancing. Do a great deal of
writing during weekends.

PERSONAL DATA

Born: 6/12/19...
Married. No children.
Height: 5'7"
Weight: 128 lbs.
Excellent health.
No relocation.

SALARY

In the $18,000s, open to negotiation if the opportunity
merits.

REFERENCES

Available on request.

Personnel Manager—
Modern Analytical Résumé

RÉSUMÉ OF
Richard W. Carlton
315 Missouri Blvd.
St. Louis, MO 64072
Date:
Phone: (314)789-5648

SUMMARY OF EXPERIENCE
Experienced in the collection, analysis and development of occupational data concerning jobs, job qualifications and worker characteristics, for facilitating selection of personnel according to the requirements of the different divisions of a company. Able to make studies of jobs being performed, and to interview workers to ascertain physical and mental characteristics in relation to procedures or services involved in the job.

OBJECTIVE
Looking for a position with a firm where the ability to interview, supervise, classify and counsel employees is needed—a firm that appreciates the practical approach and offers opportunities for material rewards.

HIGHLIGHTS OF EXPERIENCE
19...–19...
Purina Corp.
St. Louis, MO
Corporate Director of Personnel. In this position I had to find the best-qualified executives and professionals for our operations and to evaluate the self-

257

motivation and discipline of applicants. I also had to supervise ten assistants assigned to different functions of the personnel department. I had to report directly to the president of the company, and reckon with the development direction of corporate personnel policies.

19...–19...
Bainter Shoe Manufacturing Co.
Belleville, IL
Personnel Manager. In this position was responsible for supplying and keeping up to date all personnel data. This personnel data, as well as other relevant records, were kept up to date through the use of computers. The data for each employee included address, weekly or monthly earnings, absences, amount of production or sales, supervisory reports on ability, and date of and reason for termination. Compiled and prepared in final form the reports from employment records. These reports were for the use of the corporate management. Saw to it that the proper recommendation was given an employee who gave the company as a reference.

19...–19...
Baher Beer Corp.
St. Louis, MO
Assistant Personnel Manager. In this position was responsible for all personnel records. Such records were computerized and kept up to date. The records for each employee included marital status, promotions, training, assignments, nature of testing and other necessary information. These records were under constant review.

EDUCATION
  B.S. Degree in Business Administration, University of

Southern Illinois, Carbondale, IL, 19 . . . Majored in industrial psychology and took courses in personnel, which included interviewing, job analysis, industrial organization, economics. President of Delta Kappa Epsilon social fraternity. Captain of tennis team and played in intramural tennis.

EARLY BACKGROUND

Grew up in Belleville, IL. Father executive of shoe manufacturing company in Belleville. Attended public schools in Belleville and graduated from its high school. Active in high school athletics.

PROFESSIONAL MEMBERSHIPS

Delta Nu Alpha (national personnel fraternity)
Personnel Managers, St. Louis, MO
Missouri Chamber of Commerce, St. Louis, MO

OUTSIDE ACTIVITIES

Active in the operations and functions of the Settlement Society, St. Louis, MO.
Member of the St. Louis Athletic Club, St. Louis, MO.

PERSONAL INTERESTS

Studied piano for several years and still active in basic music activities—mostly classical music. Enjoy fishing, swimming and tennis.

PERSONAL DATA

Born: 7/9/19 . . .
Married, no children
Good health
Height: 5'10"
Weight: 165 lbs.
Willing to relocate, if the
offer merits

SALARY

In the $30,000s and good benefits. History of salaries available.

REFERENCES

On request, character and professional.

Programmer—Modern Analytical Résumé

RÉSUMÉ OF
Ray H. Wilson
330 East 77th St.
New York, NY 10021
Date:
Phone: (212)789-5463

SUMMARY OF EXPERIENCE

Have had long experience as a business programmer and can prepare codes, tests and documents and can analyze computer programs. Can convert generalized plans or diagrams into detailed flow charts and, from these, into symbolic computer or English-like language. Know how to develop debugging routines, and to modify and simplify programs to minimize redundancy. Possess a thorough knowledge of preparing program documentation.

OBJECTIVE

To secure a position where my experience and technical background as chief business programmer can be utilized for mutual benefit and result in appropriate remuneration and fringe benefits.

WORK-RECORD ANALYSIS

19 . . .–19 . . .
Carbondale Manufacturing Co.
Somerville, NJ
Business Programmer. Supervised a group of technicians engaged in the analysis of data-processing problems and the development and execution of programming procedures and plans. Analyzed

data-processing problems and developed systems and programs for the work to be processed. Advised employees in how to develop the more difficult programming applications.

19...–19...
Commercial Data Processing Co.
New York, NY
Computer-Program Analyst. In this position, I gained considerable experience supervising the work of a large force during the day shift. My duties required that I analyze new problems to be given to the computer. This necessitated a careful examination of each problem and the necessary steps to be taken toward a solution. A considerable part of my time was used in this preliminary analysis of problems.

19...–19...
Data Analysis and Processing Corp.
Long Island City, NY
Computer Programmer. Had to write detailed instructions for each job and to list, in logical order, the steps the machine had to follow to solve a problem. Arranged the order to follow so as to secure the information needed by the customer. Had to check the operation of each program to be sure the instructions were correct and would produce the desired information. Debugging was one of my major duties in this job.

EDUCATIONAL BACKGROUND
Northwestern University, Technological Institute, Evanston, IL. B.S. in Industrial Engineering, June 19... Majored in programming, basic engineering, basic science and mathematics, and technical design. Financed education with family allowance and part-time work.

EARLY BACKGROUND

Grew up in Oak Park, IL. Son of an electrical engineer with Crane & Co. Attended public schools and graduated from Oak Park High School in 19 . . . Active in sports; played intramural football. Member of Science Club. Worked during summer as camp helper.

PROFESSIONAL MEMBERSHIPS

American Management Association, New York, NY

American Federation of Information Processing Societies, Montvale, NJ

American Society of Electrical Engineering, New York, NY

PERSONAL

Enjoy tennis, golf, fishing. Have traveled in Mexico, Brazil and Argentina.

OUTSIDE ACTIVITIES

Member of Board of Directors, Y.M.C.A., New York, NY.

Member of Society of Friends of the Industrial Museum of Chicago, Chicago, IL.

PERSONAL DATA

Born: 7/6/19 . . .
Married, 2 children
Height: 5'11"
Weight: 175 lbs.
Licensed as professional
engineer

SALARY

In the $30,000s, with opportunity for promotion and generous fringe benefits. History of salaries available.

REFERENCES

Character and professional references available on request.

Publishing Controller—
Modern Analytical Résumé

RÉSUMÉ OF
Julius B. Monroe
315 Hunters Dr.
Cherry Hill, NJ 08003
Date:
Phone: (201)678-3456

SUMMARY OF EXPERIENCE

Have extensive experience in the techniques of cost-effective promotion on a scale that can adjust to the budget requirements of a board of directors. Am familiar with control techniques that have been effective and successful. Am able to supervise personnel operations according to formal structures and rules; can devise a total procedures guide as well as a method for executing policy decisions and enforcing deadline discipline with a minimum of conflict; and know how to improve coordination through establishing schedules.

OBJECTIVE

Am seeking a position as treasurer-controller of a substantial company, where a demonstrated record of high competence as a corporate finance officer can be fully utilized. Am seeking a connection with a publishing company that does more than $20 million in gross sales yearly.

EXPERIENCE HIGHLIGHTS
19...–19...
Aulick, Epstein Publishing Co.
Sommerville, NJ

Executive Manager and Controller. The above is a medium-sized book-publishing house. My duties here were to simplify the functions of management operations and to look into and correct the financial and promotional aspects of the books published. To meet these problems I organized a routine organization plan for the overall functions of the company that is still in use. In a number of ways, this plan was helpful in expanding the company's business.

19...–19...
Murray Hill Publishing Co.
New York, NY
Book-Publishing Manager. Among my responsibilities in this firm was the need to know the cost of each function. This was accomplished by means of controlling strategy through the budget, by establishing stronger cost controls with reference to pricing, forecasting sales and projecting cash flow, and by refashioning many of the operations. Close supervision of these areas helped the company to a considerable extent in achieving prosperity with less friction.

19...–19...
Murray Hill Publishing Co.
New York, NY
Book-Market Analysis Manager. This position required me to plan, analyze and determine growing markets for the books published. In performing these duties I was able to

Identify the marketing channels for reaching the market
Determine sales goals and methods
Develop the best marketing channels to reach these goals

Establish a promotional plan based on sound strategy
Develop a comprehensive marketing time schedule
Monitor sales response and analyze profit aspects

EDUCATION

B.S. Degree in Economics, June 19 . . . , New York University, School of Business Administration, New York, NY. The course placed special emphasis on marketing, accounting, statistics, English and psychology, and included specialized studies in such areas as financial statements, their analysis, and cost accounting. Expenses were partially financed through scholarships and loans from the government, together with summer jobs and part-time employment while in college.

EARLY BACKGROUND

Grew up in Great Neck, L.I., NY. Father an executive with Du Pont Securities Corp. Educated in public schools, and prepared for college at Great Neck High School. Member of the Science Club. Played intramural football, and have done considerable traveling in foreign countries.

PROFESSIONAL AFFILIATIONS

American Marketing Association, Chicago, IL
Conference Board, Inc., New York, NY
American Management Accounting Society, New York, NY

PERSONAL INTERESTS

Active in local politics and community affairs. During

the last five years very active in annual Red Cross drive for funds. Enjoy horseback riding and playing tennis.

PERSONAL DATA
Born: 19 . . .
Married, 2 children
Height: 5'10"
Weight: 160 lbs.
Excellent health
Willing to relocate, if
    opportunity merits

SALARY
In the $30,000s, with good benefits. History of salaries available.

REFERENCES
Available on request.

Securities Salesman—
Modern Analytical Résumé

RÉSUMÉ OF

Edward B. Hinkel
323 East 73rd Street
New York, NY 10036
Date:
Phone: (212)345-9823

SUMMARY OF EXPERIENCE

Have had five years of experience during which I acquired a background in securities and related areas. This background made it possible for me to explain the meaning of stock-market terms and trading practices to prospective investors. With prospective customers who already possessed a variety of holdings and were therefore more knowledgeable, was always ready with practical and seasoned suggestions and advice on the purchase or sale of a particular security, or on investments for either capital growth or income over a period of years.

OCCUPATIONAL OBJECTIVE

To be placed in charge of large portfolios that would enable me to use my experience and to exercise my judgment for larger incomes.

WORK-RECORD ANALYSIS

19 . . . to present
New York Aulick Corporation
New York, NY
Portfolio Manager. Study industries with regard to their kind of management and their investment pos-

sibilities. Analyze industries of a specialized nature as to their future, and prepare charts and graphs showing price fluctuations. Predict future price movements of stocks or bonds, based on my studies.

Observe the activities of the stock exchange and foresee price trends in accord with economic changes. Am very successful in my work, having gained substantial profits for the different accounts I have handled. Currently running over $30 million; clientele consists of individuals and organizations.

19 . . . to 19 . . .
Securities and Bonds Buying Service, Inc.
New York, NY

Securities Salesman. Initiated buying and selling transactions and relayed orders through my firm's offices to the floor of the securities exchange. When there was an over-the-counter transaction, I sent the order to the firm's trading department. When the buying or selling transaction was completed, notified the customer to that effect, along with the final price paid or received.

19 . . . to 19 . . .
Securities Representative. In this position I had daily dealings with customers who were interested in speculation and in profits in short time. These customers were interested in securities that were likely to rise in price quickly, and hence result in a short-term margin of profit.

In this job, furnished information to the client about the advantages and disadvantages of each kind of investment with regard to the client's objectives. Always had information at hand about prices on different stocks that the customer would be interested in.

EDUCATIONAL BACKGROUND

M.B.A.—Finance, Graduate School of Business, Columbia University, New York, NY. Majored in finance, taking additional courses in new-enterprise management, international economics, and application of computer techniques to financial management.

B.A.—Economics, Brooklyn College, Brooklyn, NY. All my courses at college were directed toward a strong financial background and financial research. Graduated with honors.

PROFESSIONAL LICENSES

New York securities license, New York, NY
National Association of Securities Dealers license

EARLY BACKGROUND

Grew up in Smithtown, NY. Father connected with the foreign operations of a multinational corporation. Attended public schools and prepared for college at Hill High School, Huntington, NY. Took active part in athletics. Member of the Debating Club. Worked in stockbroker's office during the summers.

PROFESSIONAL AFFILIATIONS

National Association of Security Dealers, Washington, DC
Put and Call Brokers & Dealers Association, Inc., New York, NY

OUTSIDE ACTIVITIES

Active in community affairs. Member of political party.

PERSONAL DATA
    Born: 19 . . .
    Married, one child
    Last physical, 19 . . .
    Height: 6'0"
    Weight: 170 lbs.
    Will relocate
    Church affiliation: active
        member, Our
        Redeemer Lutheran
        Church

SALARY
    In the $30,000s with fringe benefits, open to negotiation. History of salaries available.

REFERENCES
    Personal and business, available on request.

Soil Scientist—Modern Analytical Résumé

RÉSUMÉ OF
   Harry E. Billings
   999 Albion Street
   Denver, CO 80220
   Date:
   Phone: (303)786-4598

SUMMARY OF EXPERIENCE
   During ten years of work as a soil scientist I acquired experience in the physical, chemical and biological characteristics and behavior of soils.

OCCUPATIONAL OBJECTIVE
   To secure a position as soil scientist where my long experience as soil scientist together with my educational background can be of use to my employer and the community.

WORK-RECORD ANALYSIS
   19 . . . to present
   Soil Conservation Service
   Denver, CO
   Soil Scientist. Have been in charge of the classification of soils in Colorado. This classification is based on research. Its purpose is to determine whether the soil can produce crops, grasses and trees, and whether it is suitable as a foundation for buildings and other structures.

   19 . . . to 19 . . .
   Soil Conservation Service
   Denver, CO
   Soil Conservationist. Planned and helped in develop-

273

ing the means of preventing soil erosion, of moisture conservation and of sound land use. This involved surveying and investigating the causes of erosion and studying possible preventive measures. In cooperation with farmers and ranchers, prepared a soil-conservation plan intended for the use and treatment of the land.

19 . . . to 19 . . .
Soil Conservation Service
Denver, CO
Assistant Soil Conservationist. Among the major duties required in this position were the preparation of maps based on aerial photographs. These helped to plot the individual features of the soil and provided information as to ownership lines, field boundaries, roads and other conspicuous features.

EDUCATIONAL BACKGROUND
Denver University, Denver, CO. Obtained a B.S. in soil science. Majored in earth science.

EARLY BACKGROUND
Grew up in Denver, CO. Father a chemist for Colorado Oil Co. Attended public schools, prepared for college at George Washington High School, Denver, CO. Active in athletics and member of the Chemical Club.

PROFESSIONAL AFFILIATIONS
American Society of Agronomy, Madison, WI
National Ass'n of Conservation Districts, Washington, DC

PERSONAL INTERESTS
Community affairs and national and local politics. At present have undertaken studies for an advanced degree in soil science.

274

OUTSIDE ACTIVITIES
Swimming and tennis. Music appreciation and reading technical soil-conservation literature.

PERSONAL DATA
Born: 3/17/19 . . .
Excellent health
Good vision
Last physical: 19 . . .
Height: 5'9"
Weight: 150 lbs.

SALARY
In the $25,000s, plus fringe benefits. History of salaries available on request.

REFERENCES
Personal and professional references on request.

Training and Retraining Director—Modern Analytical Résumé

RÉSUMÉ OF

Herman M. Thorton
140 Marlton Pike East
Cherry Hill, NJ 08034
Date:
Phone: (201)765-2389

SUMMARY OF EXPERIENCE

Possess extensive background and experience as a personnel job classifier, interviewer, and training and retraining supervisor; duties include formulating plans, developing programs and administering projects to provide additional training or retraining of employees. Know how to cooperate and communicate with executive personnel in charge of human resources, and by means of this cooperation can exercise the know-how for installing new projects, for discontinuing others and for interviewing and selecting new staff members from within the organization itself. In the exercise of these duties, can assume the selection or preparation of the appropriate books, pamphlets and guidelines to be used as texts in the conduct of the different programs.

OCCUPATIONAL OBJECTIVE

To be connected with a corporation that maintains a continuing training and retraining program for staff members and regular employees. Am interested in a connection where the administration and supervision of such programs for raising the performance quality of the personnel (whether through clerical, sales or promotional programs, or specialized workshops for executives) can be conducted through one central point among the different plants in the different areas of the country. The specialized workshops for executive personnel are of particular importance in that through them, executives are supplied with all necessary information regarding new installations of machinery and changes in processes, policies and so forth. I am looking for a company that needs extensive staff development, and whose present staff size merits the acquisition of an experienced training and retraining director.

HIGHLIGHTS OF EXPERIENCE

19 . . . to present

American Pharmaceutical & Chemical Corp.

Somerville, NJ

Training and Retraining Director. As a training and retraining director with this multinational corporation, my responsibilities include planning, designing and implementing structured programs. Programs that help personnel discipline have been successfully managed and conducted for various facets of the company under my supervision. Among my other responsibilities are the organization, review, analysis and development of sound employee relations, policies and procedures, and the use of human resources for broad labor-relations programs.

19 . . .–19 . . .

Hoffman LaRoche, Inc.

Nutley, NJ

Employment Interviewer. Interviewed applicants to determine their suitability for employment with the company. Recorded the impressions and information gained from interviews with applicants, and evaluated these to determine employment possibilities. Administered tests, interpreted their results, prepared ratings on applicants and made recommendations for future consideration of those not immediately accepted for employment. Was in a position to supply information to applicants regarding company and union policies, duties, responsibilities, working conditions, hours, pay and promotion opportunities.

19 . . .–19 . . .
Hoffman La Roche, Inc.
Nutley, NJ.
Personnel Job Analyst. Studied jobs being performed and interviewed workers and supervisory personnel to ascertain physical and mental requirements as related to materials, products, processes, subject matter and services involved. Collected, analyzed and developed occupational data concerning jobs, job requirements and worker characteristics to facilitate personnel administration and supply information.

EDUCATION

Cornell University Statutory Colleges, Ithaca, NY.
M.S. in labor relations, June 19 . . . Took advanced courses in labor relations, industrial relations, human resources, community activities, and job interviewing and testing. Thesis: "Human Resources and American Industry."

Cornell University Statutory Colleges, Ithaca, NY. B.S. in industrial relations, June 19 . . . Majored in industrial relations and personnel. Other subjects included humanities, social sciences, management administration. Financed education with family allowance and part-time work.

278

EARLY BACKGROUND

Grew up in Cherry Hill, NJ. Son of a corporation lawyer. Attended public schools in Cherry Hill and graduated from Ridgewood High School, Ridgewood, NJ. Member of wrestling team during last two years. Active in other sports, played intramural football. Worked during summers as camp counselor.

PROFESSIONAL AFFILIATIONS

American Society of Industrial Engineers, New York, NY

Society for Industrial Psychologists, New York, NY

American Management Association, New York, NY

PERSONAL INTERESTS

Have traveled in Mexico, Brazil, France and North Africa. Enjoy fishing and tennis.

OUTSIDE ACTIVITIES

Member of the Community Chest, Cherry Hill, NJ.

PERSONAL DATA

Married, 2 children
Excellent health
Height: 5'11"
Weight: 190 lbs.
Willing to relocate if
    opportunity merits

SALARY

In the $30,000s plus benefits and promotion potential. (History of salaries available.)

REFERENCES

Available on request.

9

Guide to Types of Résumés for Leading Occupations

The following pages contain an alphabetical listing of more than four hundred current occupations (including the professions) in the United States.

Find your speciality in the list, or locate the one most similar to it. Next to each occupation is an *initial* indicating the recommended type of résumé: B, basic; C, chronological; F, functional; and M, modern analytical. The *number* appearing after the initial refers to the page where the sample résumé will be found. An asterisk signifies that a résumé has been prepared for that occupation. The other résumés serve as a general guide to be followed. For example:

> Agricultural Engineer, M
> Aeronautical Technician, C
> Industrial Designer,* F (155)
> Assembler, B

Details for the preparation of the four categories are given in chapters 5, 6, 7 and 8, which describe the various forms. Besides studying the individual résumé cited, read again the whole chapter outlining the presentation of your background.

Of course you are at liberty to choose any type of résumé you prefer. We have simply mentioned the type presently considered most appropriate to specific fields of work. Reviewing the chapter as a whole will doubtless spark additional ideas on how to enlarge or further adapt your own assemblage of pertinent facts regarding your capabilities.

Your résumé is your most important tool in your job-hunting efforts. No matter what type of job you are seeking—professional, semiprofessional, management, white collar, blue collar, clerical or sales—the résumé will serve as strong evidence of your abilities, and of your willingness to use these abilities in your job.

— A —

Account Executive, M
Accountant Assistant,* C (83)
Accountant, Management,* M (187)
Actuarial Technician, C
Actuary, M
Administrative Assistant,* M (191)
Administration Manager, M
Advertising-Art Production Manager,* F (194)
Advertising Manager,* M (193)
Advertising Copywriter, M
Advertising Production Manager, M
Aeronautical Engineer,* M (197)
Aeronautical Technician, C
Agricultural Engineer, M
Agricultural-Engineering Technician, C

Agricultural-Marketing Technician, C
Agricultural Technician, C
Agronomist, M
Air-Conditioning Technician,* C (85)
Aircraft-Accessories Salesman, M
Aircraft Mechanic,* C (87)
Aircraft Pilot (or Copilot),* M (201)
Airline Hostess, C
Airline-Reservations Clerk, C
Air-Traffic Controller, C
Animal Research and Development Technician, C
Anthropologist, M
Appraiser, C
Architect, M
Architectural Engineer, F
Art Production Manager, F
Artist, F
Assembler, B
Astronomer, M
Athletic Director, M
Atomic and Nuclear Technician, C
Atomic Scientist, M
Attorney, M
Auditor, M
Automobile Mechanic,* B (62)
Automobile Painter, B
Automobile-Production Technician, C

— B —

Bacteriologist, M
Bank Clerk, C
Bank Officer,* M (205)
Bank Teller,* C (89)
Bilingual Secretary,* M (209)
Billing Clerk, M

Bindery Technician, F
Biochemical Technician,* C (92)
Biochemist, M
Biologist, M
Biomedical Engineer, M
Blacksmith, C
Boilermaker Technician, C
Bookkeeper, C
Botanist, M
Broadcast Technician, C
Budget Analyst, M
Building-Materials Salesman, F
Building Superintendent, M
Business-Machines Operator, C
Business-Machines Service Technician,* C (94)
Business Manager, M
Buyer,* M (212)

— C —

Calculator and Computer Service Technician, C
Camp Counselor, C
Carpenter (Building),* B (64)
Cartographer, M
Caseworker, F
Cashier, C
Cataloger, M
Ceramic Engineer, M
Ceramic Technician, C
Certified Public Accountant, M
Chef, C
Chemical Engineer,* M (215)
Chemical Research and Development Technician, C
Chemist, M
Chiropractor, C

— D —

Dairy-Products Technician, C
Data-Processing Equipment Operator,* C (99)
Data-Processing Supervisor, C
Demonstrator, C
Dental Hygienist Technician, C
Dental Laboratory Technician, C
Dentist, F
Department-Store Manager, M
Design Engineer,* M (229)
Detective, C
Die Maker Technician, B
Diesel-Equipment Salesman, C
Dietitian,* F (149)
Direct-Mail Manager, F
Disbursement Clerk, C
Doorman, C
Draftsman, M
Dramatic Coach, M

— E —

Economic Analyst, M
Economist, M
Editor, M
Editorial Assistant, M
Electrical Engineer, M
Electrical-Technology Technician, C
Electrician (Construction),* C (106)
Electric-Powerhouse Technician, B
Electrocardiograph Technician,* C (101)
Electroencephalographic Technician,* C (103)
Electromechanical Technician, C
Electronic-Communications Technician, C
Electronic-Computer Supervisor, C

Electronic-Data-Processing Analyst, C
Electronics Engineer, C
Electronics Technician, C
Electroplater,* C (108)
Elementary School Teacher, M
Employee-Training Director, M
Employment Counselor, M
Engineer, Professional, M
Engineering Designer, M
Engineering Technician, C
English Teacher, M
Environmentalist, M
Estimator, M
Executive Secretary,* M (232)
Export and Import Assistant, M
Export and Import Manager, M

— F —

Factory Manager, M
Family Service Counselor, M
Farm-Business Technician C
Farm-Equipment Salesman, M
Fashion Designer, M
Figure Clerk, C
File Clerk, B
Finance, Executive Assistant, M
Finance, Vice-President, M
Financial Analyst, M
Financial Manager, M
Food Chemist, M
Food-Processing-Equipment Salesman, M
Food-Processing Technician, C
Food Scientist, M
Food-Services Specialist, C
Foreign-Language Teacher, M

Foreign-Marketing Manager,* M (235)
Foreign-Operations Assistant, M
Foreign-Operations Executive, M
Foreman, C
Foreman Auto Mechanic, B
Forester, C
Forestry-Products Technician, C
Free-Lance Artist, F
Full-Charge Bookkeeper, C
Fund Raiser,* F (152)
Furniture Upholsterer, C

— G —

General Office Worker, B
Geographer, M
Geological Engineer, M
Geological Technician, C
Geologist, M
Geophysical Technician, C
Geophysicist, M
Graphic-Arts Technician, C
Guard and Watchman, B
Guidance Counselor, M

— H —

Handicap Worker, C
Health-Services Administrator, C
Heating-Equipment Sales and Service Technician, C
Histologic Technician, C
Home Economist, M
Horticulture Research and Development Technician, C
Horticulturist, M
Hospital Administrator, M
Hospital Attendant, C

Hostess, C
Hotel Clerk,* C (110)
Hotel Front-Office Clerk, C
Hotel Manager, M
Housekeeper, B
House-Organ Editor, M
Human-Resources Executive,* F (155)

— I —

Industrial Designer,* F (158)
Industrial Engineer,* M (238)
Industrial-Machinery Technician, C
Industrial Physician, M
Industrial-Production Technician, C
Industrial-Relations Assistant, M
Industrial-Relations Manager, M
Industrial Salesman, M
Industrial-Traffic Manager,* M (241)
Information-Systems Specialist, M
Inspector (Manufacturing), C
Instrumentation Engineer, C
Instrumentation Technician,* C (112)
Instrument Maker (Mechanical), C
Insurance Agent and Broker, C
Insurance-Claim Adjuster, C (115)
Interior-Claims Adjuster, C
Interior Designer, M
Internal Auditor, M
International-Marketing Analyst,* M (244)
International-Sales Executive, M
Interpreter, F
Interviewer, M
Inventory-Control Manager, C
Investigator, C
Investment Analyst, M

—J—

Job-Guidance Counselor, M
Journalist, M
Journeyman Carpenter, B
Junior Accountant, C
Junior Copywriter,* M (247)

—K—

Keypunch Operator, C
Kindergarten Teacher, M

—L—

Laboratory Technician, C
Labor-Relations Manager, M
Ladies' Shoe Buyer, M
Landscape Architect,* F (161)
Landscaper, F
Lawyer, M
Layout and Visualization Artist, F
Layout Man, M
Legal Aide, M
Librarian, M
Linotype Operator, C
Livestock-Production Technician, C

—M—

Machine Assembler, B
Machinery-Maintenance Technician, B
Machine-Tool Operator, B
Machinist, B
Maintenance Superintendent, M
Management Accountant, M

290

Management Aide, M
Management Science Specialist, M
Management Trainee, C
Manufacturer's Inspector, C
Manufacturer's Salesman,* M (251)
Manufacturing Engineer, M
Manuscript Editor,* M (254)
Marketing-Research Assistant,* C (117)
Marketing-Research Manager, M
Marketing-Research Technician, C
Mason, B
Mathematical Technician, C
Mathematician, M
Mechanic, M
Mechanical Engineer,* M (56)
Mechanical-Engineering Technician, M
Media Director, M
Medical Engineer Technician, C
Medical-Laboratory Worker, C
Medical-Record Administrator, C
Medical Social Worker, M
Medical Technologist, C
Medical Writer, M
Medical X-Ray Technician, C
Merchandising Manager, F
Merchandising Technician, C
Metallurgical Engineer, M
Metallurgical Technician, C
Meteorological Technician, C
Meteorologist, M
Methods Engineer, M
Microbiologist, M
Milk-Plant-Equipment Technician, C
Millwright, B
Mining Engineer, M
Model, F

Molder, F
Motel Manager, M
Motion-Picture Projectionist, B
Musician, F

— N —

Newspaper Reporter, M
Nurse, Practical,* C (119)
Nurse, Registered,* F (164)

— O —

Occupational Therapist Technician, M
Oceanographer, M
Oceanographer Technician, C
Office-Machine Operator, B
Office Manager, M
Office Worker, C
Optical-Laboratory Mechanic, C
Optical-Laboratory Technician, C
Optometrist, M
Ornamental-Metal Estimator, C
Osteopathic Physician, M
Overseas-Operations Executive Vice-President, M
Overseas Production Manager,* F (167)
Overseas Regional Manager, M

— P —

Painter, F
Paramedical Aide, C
Patternmaker Technician,* C (122)
Payroll Clerk, C
Personal-Trust Officer, M
Personnel Interviewer, M

Personnel Manager,* M (257)
Petroleum Engineer, M
Petroleum Geologist, M
Pharmaceuticals Salesman, M
Pharmacist, M
Photoengraver,* C (124)
Photographer, M
Physical-Education Teacher, M
Physical Therapist, C
Physician, M
Physicist, M
Physiotherapist, C
Piano Teacher, M
Placement Officer, M
Planning and Development Manager, M
Plant Breeder Technician, C
Playground Director, M
Plumber and Pipefitter Technician, B
Police Officer, M
Postal Clerk, C
Poultry-Production Technician, C
Power-Truck Operator,* B (70)
Press Agent, C
Principal, High School, M
Printing Pressman, B
Private Accountant, M
Private-Duty Nurse, C
Production Planner Assistant,* C (126)
Product Manager, M
Programmer,* M (261)
Programmer, Business, M
Psychologist, M
Public Accountant, M
Public-Health Laboratory Technician, C
Public-Health Technician, C
Publicity Director, M

Public-Relations Assistant,* C (128)
Public-Relations Manager, M
Publisher's Salesman, F
Publishing Controller,* M (265)
Purchasing Manager, M

— Q —

Quality-Control Manager, M

— R —

Radio and Television Announcer, F
Radiology Technician,* F (170)
Real-Estate Agent and Broker, F
Recreation Director, M
Recruiter, Personnel, M
Registered Nurse, F
Rehabilitation Counselor, M
Reporter, M
Research Officer, C
Reservation Clerk, C
Restaurant Manager, M
Retail-Sales Clerk, M
Retail-Store Manager, M
Retraining Director, M
Rewrite Man, M

— S —

Sales Clerk, C
Salesman, F
Sales-Promotion Manager,* F (172)
Sanitation Technician, B
School Administrator, M
School Counselor, C

Science and Technical Translator, M
Science Teacher, M
Scientific-Data-Processing Technician, C
Secondary School Teacher, C
Secretary-Stenographer, M
Securities Salesman,* M (269)
Security Officer, C
Sheet-Metal Worker,* B (72)
Shipping and Receiving Clerk, C
Social Worker, M
Sociologist, M
Soil Reclamation and Conservation Technician, C
Soil Scientist,* M (273)
Sound-Equipment Sales and Service Technician, C
Speech Pathologist and Audiologist, M
State-Police Officer, M
Stationary Engineer, M
Stationary Fireman (Boiler), B
Statistical Clerk, C
Statistician, M
Stenographer and Secretary, M
Stock Clerk, C
Stock-Market Broker, M
Supermarket Manager, F
Supervisor, M
Surveyor Assistant,* C (130)
Switchboard Operator, C
Systems Analyst, M
Systems Analyst Technician, C

— T —

Tabulating-Equipment Operator,* C (132)
Tax Accountant, M
Teacher, M
Technical Writer, M

Telephone Operator, C
Textile Designer Technician, F
Textile-Equipment Technician, C
Tool and Die Maker,* B (74)
Topographical Draftsman,* C (135)
Topographic Surveyor Technician, C
Traffic Manager, M
Training and Retraining Director,* M (276)
Training Supervisor, M
Translator, M
Transportation Clerk, C
Travel Agent, C
Treasurer-Controller, M
TV and Radio Announcer,* F (175)
Typewriter Sales and Service Technician, C
Typist, M

— U —

Underwriter, C
Urban Planner Engineer, F

— V —

Vending-Machine Service Technician, C
Veterinarian, M
Vocational Teacher, M

— W —

Waitress, B
Water-Sanitation Technician, C
Welder,* B (76)
Wildlife and Conservation Technician, C
Woodwork-Equipment Sales and Service Technician, C

— Z —

Zoologist, M

Part 3

Using the Résumé to Get a Job

10

Job-Searching
Techniques

Starting to Look for a Job

Under the best of circumstances, looking for a job is a difficult undertaking. Despite the difficulties, however, millions of adults do get jobs every year. While job-search methods are certainly important, other factors such as skill, experience and motivation must be considered.

It is necessary to bear in mind that economic conditions very much affect the market in which a job search is undertaken. Faced with the competition brought about by unfavorable economic conditions, it is necessary for the job seeker to make more intensive use of informal methods, along with more costly formal methods, such as private employment agencies. Of course, when jobs are plentiful, the job seeker may feel that it isn't necessary to spend money on employment agencies or similar help.

When you decide to change jobs and are ready to look for one, you must contact all possible places of employment and all persons who can help you. The more places you contact and the more people you see, the better will be your chance of finding work.

As a start, register at your local employment office. This office receives many requests for workers for many different kinds of jobs. It also tries to contact employers to find suitable jobs for applicants. Talk to friends and neighbors—they may know about job openings. It would be especially helpful to talk with those who do the same kind of work you do—you might get some first-hand information by "talking shop."

Read and answer the "want ads" in newspapers and trade journals. If hiring in your occupation is done through a union, contact yours and, at the same time, either by letter or in person, companies that employ people in your kind of work. You will find such companies listed in your classified telephone directory, or in local and state industrial directories. Inquire at the job-placement office of your school, if it has one, and at other places such as the "Y."

If you want to become an apprentice, consult the local state employment service office and ask about training opportunities for skilled trades. Contact officials in industries, in labor unions and in trade associations. Get in touch with an apprenticeship information center, if there is one in your city, and with members of local joint apprenticeship committees. You should also contact the Bureau of Apprenticeship and Training, U.S. Department of Labor, or your state apprenticeship agency, about apprenticeship opportunities in your area. To get federal, state or local-government jobs, you will have to apply for and take a civil service examination. Obtain an application blank from your post office or your local civil service office. You will be notified when to appear for the test, and after you take it you will receive word regarding your score.

Executive Search Service

In your strategy for changing jobs, use discretion. If your present employers find out that you are looking for another job, they may resent it. Their resentment is a fact of life in the business world, and not something you should overlook. Also, when another company is considering you, it may be for a job that is held by someone else.

A popular way to secure an intermediary is to turn your problem over to an executive-recruiting service. The better services are fully aware of the need for secrecy and for you, their client, to be happily employed.

Executive-recruiting firms work on behalf of client companies who do, in fact, pay the necessary fees. When a client company needs someone—a man or a woman—it quietly commissions the recruiting service to find the right person. The fee usually averages 20 to 25 percent of the first year's total pay for the job in question. Thus, a job paying a salary of $30,000 a year would necessitate a fee of at least $6,000 to the recruiting service.

There was a time when the recruiting services faced certain difficulties in its search for the right person for a particular job. Today, the services need look no further than their own files. They feed a description of the person who is needed into a computer, then they contact the individuals whose cards are selected by the machine. Your card may be among those selected simply because you visited or wrote the service, and left a good résumé of your qualifications with them.

One leading executive-recruiting service that regularly receives about one thousand résumés each month from executives transfers the information from the résumé to computer file cards. If you are right on your toes, you won't be content with simply supplying the recruiting service with information for their massive files. You will keep in constant touch with them to make sure that you are not just a name in a file card and are not overlooked.

Search services ordinarily handle prospects who command at least $20,000 a year, since their fee is related to the salary offered. However, in some instances, they will consider someone at a $15,000 salary, if the applicant is young and shows initiative and promise. Such a "comer" will no doubt, at another time, seek higher-paying jobs that can yield higher fees to the recruiting service.

Sometimes, when a recruiting service is reluctant to take you on, it may not be because you are unworthy of its efforts, but because it is handling assignments for your present company without your knowledge. It is a matter of ethics for the service not to lure employees from a client company. This can sometimes have unusual results. Many large companies that are well staffed with executive talent consider it ordinary business prudence to offer assignments to the service, so as to avoid the possibility of being raided by it at some future date. On the other hand, some major recruiting services will not take on this type of corporation as a client, for the reason that they can make more money raiding these companies for other clients.

The prevalence of executive search firms has resulted in a significant emphasis on "the executive look." These search firms undertake to find a candidate they can place with their client in order to make money. Thus, they tend to look for a person who is a "successful package," part of which is the "look" of an executive. This, incidentally, has resulted in the charge that the search services have become typecasting bureaus.

If you are relatively young, bear in mind that you will most likely change companies several times, if and when you become dissatisfied with particular jobs. With each change, any one of your prospective employers will very likely look closely into your background and contact at least two of your former employers. It would be wise, therefore, to make sure that the employers and associates you leave think and speak well of you.

Personnel searchers or managers almost always see the applicant's résumé before arranging for an interview. When your résumé and letter are well prepared, they can be a helpful stepping-stone in obtaining the right job at the right salary for you.

In addition to sending your recruiter a copy of your résumé, enclose a letter covering these points:

(1) The kind of work you want and can do.
(2) The salary range you will accept.
(3) Whether you are willing to relocate.
(4) When you are available for employment.
(5) Suggest possibilities for arranging an interview.
(6) Your willingness to abide by the terms of a contract—if any—given by the recruiter.
(7) Your willingness to accept collect calls or telegrams, and where.
(8) Offer to submit a photograph of yourself. This is not always required since it is forbidden in some states, but you may do so voluntarily.

The Private Employment Agency

The employment agency specializes in finding jobs

for people and people for jobs. A person seeking employment is in the position of an artist who needs a resourceful agent to sell his talents. The private employment agency offers diversified opportunities and large markets for selection. In many cases, the private agency can secure entry for a job seeker into companies that are difficult of access. Thus, like the executive-recruiting service, the agency operates as middleman between employer and the job seeker.

As a qualified applicant, you can usually depend on a reliable private agency to estimate your aptitudes and skills, classify you for the different positions in which you are likely to excel and give you occupational advice and actual leads.

Employers also receive valuable and often unrecognized services from the private employment agency. Clients sometimes fail to realize the work done by the agency before it sends an applicant for an interview. The manager of the agency must often "sell" the company to the employee and overcome such objections from him as "the location is inconvenient," "working conditions don't seem just right," or "the hours don't appeal to me." Both employer and applicant must also realize that agencies operate under regulations enforced by state or local authorities. An introduction to a prospective employer is therefore *bona fide*.

In the better agencies, the staff is apt to be quite skilled in detecting abilities and exploring the personalities of candidates, and they are equipped to do a thorough job of evaluation.

As an example, let us assume that you are the manager of the foreign department of a company doing a great deal of overseas business. You are looking for skilled employees as trainees or replacements, and you turn to a reputable employment agency. The person at the agency who handles applicants in your general area of work must have an extensive background of travel abroad, a reasonable command of foreign languages and some knowledge of international commercial skills before he can refer an applicant to you.

A further example: The agency may know that the vice-president who needs a secretary has a vile temper and is therefore looking for a mature and tranquil individual. Or let us suppose the essential requirement for someone in the media department of an advertising agency is accuracy. The placement manager in the agency takes note of a young man who has patiently worked his way through months of uncongenial work for a paint manufacturer, but—because of the young man's reputation for accuracy—gives him a chance to enter the advertising field. Even those who have acquired specialized qualifications through training and experience may find that the private employment agency is the most direct route to a prospective employer.

The practice of some companies to advertise for applicants through newspaper ads is, in the long run, much more expensive than any fee the agency may charge. Personnel departments of large companies advertise for help in newspapers and periodicals largely to improve efficiency. The time element in screening applications, reading poorly arranged résumés, eliminating the "drifters" who make a practice of answering ads, and answering letters, can be quite costly. The agency refers an applicant who has already been screened and by this means saves the client time and money.

Help Wanted

The "Help Wanted" sections of newspapers print a variety of employment offers. These are of two kinds:

the open ad, which identifies the company and its address; and the blind ad, which provides only a box number to which the applicant must write. Of course, it is better to answer the open ad that gives you the name of the company, its location and possibly some information about its business. However, the blind ad is used when firms do not want it known that they need a new employee, as this could have a disturbing effect on their staff.

Do not be taken in by attractively worded ads. Many are written only to entice applicants for jobs with many limitations. And beware of ads which ask applicants to take a course, or deposit money or buy samples. These are often a disguise for selling something.

News

Business and industrial news items in your local paper or trade magazine can offer a clue as to where you can apply for a position. You would do well to clip and save articles about the opening of new plants and offices, the enlargement of stores, factories or offices, and the development of new products. A personal item about the promotion, transfer or resignation of an employee may indicate a vacancy for which you might qualify. These items and notices are often forecasts of the need for more personnel. You can contact the personnel manager of each firm and ask about new opportunities for employment.

Friends and Acquaintances

It has been said that it's not what you know, but who you know that counts. This is undoubtedly true in many instances—and it is indeed too bad when an unqualified person is preferred over one who is better qualified because of someone's influence. We are not suggesting that you depend on "pull" to secure employment. Do not, however, overlook friends who may be of real assistance to you. One among your friends may even know of a vacancy in a company that is exactly in line with your own qualifications. Or a salesman friend may be in a particularly good position to help you, since salesmen are always seeing and speaking to people.

A note of caution: *do not pester your friends about a job*. Let them know that you are available and what you can do, and suggest how they might be of help. They are sure to appreciate your problem, since they themselves have very likely been in your situation. But if you tend to use your friends and to hound them, and make no effort on your own to find a job, they will not cooperate, and you might lose them as friends.

Selection of Companies

Another way of finding vacancies is actually to canvas companies for which you would like to work. You might make a list of these companies. A methodical review of ads in trade journals, of headings in the classified telephone directories, and of the financial and business sections of newspapers will provide you with the names of many companies in the field you desire. The chamber of commerce in many cities might help with a list of local companies that might be able to use your services.

If the firms you are interested in are in your vicinity, you might call in person and present your résumé. (Suggestions for the proper approach for an interview will appear in a later section of this manual.) It is suggested that you plan your calls a day in advance by neighborhoods, so as to save time, energy, fares and shoe leather.

The telephone might also be of help in contacting someone for a personal interview. If you use the telephone, be prepared with a short, snappy sales talk. Offer your reasons for using the telephone instead of calling in person, and have a ready answer for any turn the conversation may take. Hold the listener's attention by asking appropriate questions—and try to arrange for a personal interview.

Help from Organizations

There is currently a great deal of unemployment throughout the United States, more in some areas than in others, and mostly in the large cities. A great many reasons are being given as to the causes of this high unemployment problem. The U.S. Department of are not enough jobs available. Some job openings require skills, training and education that many people do not possess. Then there are those who are handicapped or who have other forms of disability. The situation is very complex; but whatever the reasons, one thing is certain: the longer a person is unemployed, the more difficult it is for that person to get a job.

Private industry, nonprofit organizations and our government are participating in efforts to solve the unemployment problem. The U.S. Department of Labor is particularly active in efforts toward full employment. A major thrust is the Job Opportunities in the Business Sector (JOBS) Program, which consists of a partnership between government and business working together to hire the hard-core unemployed and pay them as they train. Another approach is the Concentrated Employment Program, which provides all manpower and related services in areas where there is the most need. Out-of-school training is part of this campaign. New Careers offers experience to youths in preparing them for regular jobs. Some of these programs necessitate going into areas of unemployment instead of waiting for those without jobs to come to employment offices. Still another approach is for employers to develop jobs for those in need. In some cases employers and local agencies have set up training programs for people who don't have the necessary skills to fill certain jobs. Many of these programs are intended for young people who have little or no work experience, and who would have great difficulty in finding jobs on their own.

Since a job—especially your first one—is so important, you must not trust to blind luck. But that's just what you'll be doing if you begin your search without enough knowledge or information about jobs, about how to go about finding them and about yourself as a worker. There are many who can help you in your search. You'll be doing yourself a favor if you take advantage of the experience and knowledge that is available to you.

The State Employment Service

Every state has an employment service in your town or nearby. This office can help you find a suitable job. You should use its services.

No one looking for a job should be denied the opportunity to work because of race, color, national origin, religion, sex or age. The law and federal regulations specifically prohibit such discrimination. Strong efforts are being made by government, private industry, labor unions and community groups to bring about equal employment opportunity for everybody.

The state employment office receives requests for workers from various employers in your community. The staff is familiar with jobs that are available and with those that are more difficult to obtain. Counselors have occupational information and forecasts based on local conditions and they know the hiring requirements and wages in your area. The office also gives tests which will help you find out and measure your aptitudes and abilities. With their understanding of how to relate test scores to jobs, these counselors can help you find the work you can do best, and also put you in touch with employers.

Other kinds of assistance, such as apprenticeship or training programs, are also available through your state employment service. Some local offices have an apprenticeship information center that works closely with employers and unions. Even where the employment service has no apprenticeship information center, the personnel knows what is available for you.

If you are under 22 years of age, your employment service office may be able to help you through one of the youth opportunity centers located in large cities around the country. These centers are especially designed to help young people prepare for and find jobs.

The blue-collar or white-collar worker who may not be familiar with the preparation of a résumé must realize that under present economic conditions, a résumé is absolutely necessary. Factories and other places of business are not always within easy reach, so that the best and most direct way to reach them is by submitting a résumé, which is really a selling instrument that can help you in locating a job.

From the JOB-FLO report you can learn if there's a job in Chicago when you are jobless in Philadelphia. The U.S. Employment Service, in combination with each state employment service, issues a monthly report called "Occupations in Demand," which provides details about jobs that were most plentiful during the previous month. It is designed to depict the job-opportunity patterns month-by-month. The report may be obtained at any local employment office. JOB-FLO reports tell whether there is large demand for specific kinds of workers in a particular city or region. It also shows what the jobs pay, which industries need workers in certain occupations and how much experience or education the applicant should have.

Help from Your State Department of Labor

Both state and federal governments have laws regulating the employment of young people. The Federal Fair Labor Standards Act states that persons 16 years old and over may be employed in all occupations except those that are declared hazardous by the Secretary of Labor. There are seventeen such occupations currently declared off-limits for workers under 18 years of age. Among jobs considered hazardous are those of motor-vehicle driver and helper; operator of any power-driven hoisting machinery, including elevators; and operators of certain power-driven machines. This law sets the conditions for youths aged 14 and 15 to work outside school hours in a limited number of occupations, such as office and sales work, and certain food-service and gasoline and service jobs.

Each state has its own laws setting minimum wages, hours and conditions of work, the required school attendance, and the issuance of work permits for young people. To find out about these laws and how they might affect you, get in touch with the nearest local office of your state employment service, or write to your state department of labor, which is usually located in your state capital.

Help from Counselors, Teachers or Principals

The high school you attend is an excellent starting point in planning your future occupation. Your school counselor has vocational and personality tests to define your interests and abilities. He can help you select courses and vocational training that fit your plans and give you a real head start in looking for a job. In addition, he knows of special surveys about labor conditions that may have been issued by school or community groups in your area.

Other sources of information in your school include teachers of such special subjects as industrial arts, shorthand and art, who can give you information about jobs related to these subjects. Your school librarian, as well as your counselor, principal and teachers, may have information about jobs that you will want to investigate and consider.

Help from Your Union

Your occupational choice may make it necessary for you to talk with such knowledgeable people as union representatives, who have information about the field you want to enter. Hiring for certain positions is sometimes done directly through joint apprenticeship committees. Even if this is not the case, officials of these committees will be able to tell you about the outlook for their occupations and about their apprenticeship programs. You can also write letters to, and make appointments at, the personnel offices of employers offering the kind of work that interests you. They will have information about job requirements and work opportunities. Most appointments with federal and state governments have specific requirements, including a test for which you must apply in advance. For information about government jobs, contact your local, federal or state civil service commission office, which is usually in the local post office. The exact addresses, however, of both federal and state civil service commission offices are in your telephone directory.

Union officials, employers, and representatives of the civil service commissions are all willing to help you, but it is up to you to contact them.

Help from Local Recruiters for the Army, Air Force, Navy and Marine Corps

Advice on career and training possibilities in the armed forces is also available from recruiters who are stationed in, or regularly visit, your community. Many young men, and some young women, spend some years in the armed services. These years can be used to acquire education and training that will later open doors to interesting and well-paying civilian jobs. As far as the needs of the armed forces allow, your aptitudes, training and interests will be considered in your assignment. Naturally, you will be able to use these years to better advantage if you have made a thoughtful occupational selection before joining the armed forces.

Experience gained from military service can be useful. A recent study indicated that workers in some jobs do better and make more progress when they have had related military training. In addition, as a veteran you will receive special consideration when applying for a job. The local state employment service office has the responsibility of contacting veterans and providing them with additional services. However, even if you are a veteran, don't wait for an employment service to contact you. Visit the local state employment service office and ask for the veteran's representative. He will see that you are well taken care of.

Help from Workers in the Field that Interests You

Another way of finding out about particular jobs is to question people about their fields of work. Most people like to "talk shop" and are glad to give information to young, interested beginners. They may even know about openings in their own establishments or in other companies. If you know someone engaged in the line of work that appeals to you, ask for information. Or ask a friend or relative who might know someone who works in your field.

Part-time and Temporary Employment

Many students work from time to time while they are still in school, either after school hours or during vacations. By working part-time or during the summer, students gain experience that can be useful in obtaining full-time work after graduation. For some students, such work is an experiment. They find out what they like and don't like. In addition, many of them use the money earned from a part-time or temporary job to help meet school expenses. For others, such work is a source of extra spending money.

In many parts of the country, the state employment service cooperates with local schools, businesses and industries to set up programs that combine on-the-job training with continued education for students. These programs usually run throughout the school year and may offer the opportunity to earn credits toward high school graduation. They may also include training courses at the employer's establishment or at the school.

If you have had some part-time or temporary work, think about what you have learned and how you may use it toward choosing and obtaining a full-time job. If you are interested in on-the-job training that relates to your educational or vocational goal, see your high school counselor, teacher or principal for more information; and visit your local employment service office for additional details.

Direct-Mail Promotion

If the record of your qualifications and work history are too long for one of the forms outlined thus far, you might also use a letter. Of course, such a letter should have sales appeal and contain all pertinent information. The résumé should be prepared as shown in the personal occupational inventory for the modern analytical form.

After you have completed your résumé and accompanying "selling" letter, you must prepare a carefully compiled list of firms to whom they should be sent.

In some ways, this step is the most important of your job-seeking program. The best résumé and letter in the world will not help you if they go to the wrong firms.

The kind of paper you use, and the method of reproducing your résumé and letter must be considered very carefully. You must also give consideration to the quantity you will need, the cost of printing, reproduction and mailing.

Following is a list of directories. By going through them you can easily compile a list of prospective concerns who would be interested in what you have to offer. List these organizations and their addresses in the order of your preference. Address your letter and résumé to the personnel department:

(1) *American Firms Operating in Foreign Countries, Directory of,* 9th ed., N.Y. World Trade Academy Press/Uniworld Reference Publications, New York, 1977

(2) *College Placement Annual,* The College Placement Council, Inc., Bethlehem, Penn.

(3) *Construction Employment Guide,* 3rd ed., World Trade Academy Press, Inc., New York, 1977

(4) *Dun & Bradstreet Reference Directory* (annual), Dun & Bradstreet, New York.

(5) *Foreign Firms Operating in U.S.,* Directory of, 4th ed., World Trade Academy Press, Inc., New York, 1977

(6) *Guide to American Directories,* 7th ed., B. Klein & Co., New York, 1976

(7) *Looking for Employment in Foreign Countries* (by J. L. Angel), 6th ed., World Trade Academy Press, New York, 1972

(8) *Multinational Marketing and Employment Directory,* 7th ed., World Trade Academy Press, Inc., New York, 1977

(9) Poor's Register of Directories and Executives (annual), Standard & Poor's Corp., New York.

(10) *Thomas' Register of Manufacturers* (annual), Thomas Publishing Co., New York.

(11) *Trade Directories of the World,* Croner Publications, Queens Village, NY (Looseleaf kept up to date by an amendment service.)

11

The Covering Letter

Suggestions for Your Covering Letter

All the information as to your qualifications for the job you are seeking is in your résumé. Your covering letter accompanying the résumé should, therefore, be to the point, relaxed in manner and not too long. All you need to say in your covering letter is that you are enclosing your résumé and that you are available for an interview at any convenient time.

Actually, your covering letter is really a sort of personal introduction to the record of your working life as revealed in the résumé that accompanies it. It is different from a letter of application. Generally, when you are submitting the covering letter together with your résumé, you have a specific job in mind and for which you are applying.

In your covering letter you should make certain that you have expressed yourself in a way that will engage the attention of the reader to what you have to offer, and that will continue to hold his attention as he reads your résumé.

Following are suggestions as to how your covering letter should be arranged:

(1) The *Heading* indicates your address and the date. It appears in the upper right-hand corner. When you compose a letter on which your name and address appear in print, only the date should be typed in. The first line of the heading should be typed about 2½ inches below the top of the paper. For a shorter letter, the first line should be from two to eight spaces lower, depending on the length of the letter.

(2) The *Introductory Address* consists of the name and address of the person to whom the letter is written. Its first line is flush with the left-hand margin, about six lines below the last line of the heading. The introductory address, like the heading, should be single-spaced.

(3) The *Salutation* is your greeting and you can choose from any one of the following: "Dear Sir," "Dear Madam," "Gentlemen," "My dear Mr. . . ," "My dear Ms. . . ." The salutation is also flush with the left-hand margin, two spaces below the last line of the introductory address, and two lines above the body of the letter.

(4) The *Body of the Letter* is the message. The arrangement in the body should look well balanced on the sheet of paper. Each left-hand line should be flush, except for the first line beginning each paragraph, which you can indent a few spaces, or can leave flush also. Either way, the paragraphs should be at least two spaces apart.

(5) The *Closing* is typed two or three spaces below the last line of the body. It should be even with the top line of the heading. It should not extend beyond the right margin. Most closings are as follows: "Sincerely," "Cordially," "Yours very truly," "Yours truly."

318

(6) The *Signature:* here is where you sign your name under the closing, in pen and ink.

"Don'ts" When Writing Letters

Don't put anything in your letter that you cannot substantiate in the personal interview.

Don't write for a particular job unless you are certain you want it.

Don't use sympathy or any sense of urgency as a lever for forcing the interview.

Don't use your covering letter for any other purpose than as an adjunct to your résumé—and leave your personal, political and economic philosophy out of it.

Don't laud over personal honors or distinctions in an attempt to make a good impression.

Don't use gimmicks or any form of boasting. Forthright honesty, not trickery, will impress.

Don't address your letter to a company or a title. Use the name of a person, if possible, or the department or division that will supervise your work.

Don't buy the employer favors. Sell your own ability and talent.

Don't write overlong letters; just present the important facts. Let your résumé speak for you.

Don't mail a résumé without a covering letter.

Don't forget to polish the draft of the letter before making the final copy.

Don't forget to adapt your letter to the facts in the résumé, or the conditions that pertain to a job opportunity.

Don't use routine openings instead of probing for an expression of individuality.

Don't fail to tap what is best in your résumé by drawing attention to it.

Don't fail to close your letter with a request for a possible interview.

Don't use jargon—the simple, direct language of everyday speech is best.

Don't fail to reread your résumé and covering letter before mailing. Check appearance, grammar, spelling.

Use Action Words

Action words convey participation, involvement and accomplishment. They produce a strong impact on the reader. Avoid conventional or stereotyped words or phrases.

The following list of action words and phrases will help make your résumé and covering letter more readable and distinctive:

TRAIT APTITUDES

clerical perception
color discrimination
creative imagination
eye–hand coordination
finger dexterity
form perception

intelligence
manual dexterity
motor coordination
numerical
spatial
verbal

SKILLS AND ABILITIES

administer
analyze
assist
communicate
compose
conceive an ideal
contribute
create
create copy
create profit

delegate
develop
economize
implement
indoctrinate
innovate
install
lead
learn
manage

organize
plan
profitability
qualify for
recruit
save money
solve problems
supervise

systematize
teach
train
understand
work in harmony
work well with others
write

ACCOMPLISHMENTS AND INVOLVEMENTS

accomplish
achieve
contribute
increase
introduce new concepts
multiple profit
multiple sales

progress
reduce
reorganize
restore profit
save
sold

EXPERIENCE AND BACKGROUND

achievement
capable
complete
comprehensive
consistent
demonstrably
diversified
effective
experienced
extensive
familiarity
growth
in-depth

intensive
intimate
producer
progress
progressive
record
regulation
scope
solid
successful
thoroughgoing
varied
wide

FORTIFYING WORDS FOR YOUR SENTENCE

analyze
conduct
create
design
develop
direct
expand
implement
invent
manage
negotiate

organize
plan
present
profits
reduce costs
research
sold
supervise
train
wrote

FORTITUDE APTITUDES

coolness
courage
endurance
firmness
intrepidity

power
resolution
spirit
strength
vigor

PERSONAL QUALIFICATIONS

able
accustomed
administrator
analytical
bilingual
boldness
broad gauge
capable
communication skills
competent
conceptual
contributor
controlled

coordinator
creative
dauntless
dedicate
develop
distinguish
dynamic
educate
effective
efficient
enterprise
exceptional
executive

322

fearless
forbearance
gallantly
harmonious
imaginative
indoctrinate
ingenious
innovative
inventive
leader
manager
motivate
motivator
negotiator
organizer
outstanding
patience

planner
possess
producer
reliable
resistant
responsible
schooled
skilled
specialist
strategist
stress
student of
superior
talented
trained
traveled
used to

Sample Covering Letters

Administration Executive Vice-President

John R. Roopper
211 East 70th Street
New York, NY 10021
(212)755-2386

Mr. Don M. Caldwell
Human Relations Manager
Blake Manufacturing Co.
529 West 36th Street
New York, NY 10001

Dear Mr. Caldwell:

The most important qualification and function of an Executive Vice-President is the ability to plan well and soundly, and then to imbue his staff with the spirit of teamwork. In other words, ADMINISTRATION.

The attached résumé will briefly highlight my experience for the past fifteen years. You will note that I started in the shops, during the summer vacations, and progressed steadily up through the production phases of operations until I reached my present goal.

During my four years as Executive Vice-President of the company, I have reduced costs, installed new methods, increased sales, increased the capital investment by some 700% and built a smoothly running organization.

324

The reason why I am contacting you is that my present connection no longer offers any challenge—there is no place for me to go—the field for the products is limited and we are currently getting more than our share of the available market.

I would appreciate the opportunity of speaking with you, at your convenience, so that we might explore just where my experience can be utilized in your present organization to increase your profits.

Looking forward to your reply with great interest.

Very truly yours,

John R. Roopper

Advertising Executive

John R. Roopper
211 East 70th Street
New York, NY 10021
(212)755-2386

Mr. Don M. Caldwell
Human Relations Manager
Blake Manufacturing Co.
519 West 36th Street
New York, NY 10001

Dear Mr. Caldwell:

The attached résumé briefly covers my career involving Sales, Advertising, Sales Promotion and, to a certain extent, Market Research. Presently employed, I am seeking a connection with a firm which will use my full abilities and where I can materially contribute to its continued success.

My present position offers no further challenge because I have been automatically stopped from further advancement within the company—a son-in-law has been taken into the firm within the past six months, as Vice-President in charge of Advertising—and while the company has assured me that I have a permanent position with them, I feel that further advancement is impossible.

I am particularly desirous of becoming associated with a concern such as yours, which has a progressive policy of Sales and Advertising and where my experience can be used to further continued growth and expansion—the addition of new products, expansion of sales effort and improvement of customer relations.

The enclosed résumé, of course, cannot take the place of a personal interview, and therefore, I would appreciate an appointment at your convenience, to discuss my experience in the light of your present or proposed plans, and how I might be of service to the company.

Your reply, with date of such appointment, is awaited with interest.

Very truly yours,

John R. Roopper

———————————————————

John R. Roopper
211 East 70th Street
New York, NY 10021
(212)755-2386

Mr. Don M. Caldwell
Human Relations Manager
B. L. Smith Corporation
529 East 52nd Street
New York, NY 10022

Dear Mr. Caldwell:

This letter is my application for a position with your company. I have just graduated from Dartmouth College with a degree in Business Administration and I am ambitious to begin working.

The enclosed résumé will give you all the pertinent facts about my education and my past record of employment. I am particularly interested in working for the Smith Corporation because the department store field has always interested me. In fact, it is the field in which I worked during my summer vacations and on Saturdays.

While most of my experience has been as salesman, I would welcome an opportunity to work in merchandising. I am anxious to learn all aspects of the work, especially with your organization.

The attached résumé indicates my capabilities. May I suggest that a personal interview, at your convenience of course, will permit both of us to explore the possibilities? Your reply, with time and place of such an appointment, will be greatly appreciated.

Very truly yours,

John R. Roopper

John R. Roopper
211 East 70th Street
New York, NY 10021
(212)755-2386

Mr. Don M. Caldwell,
Human Relations Manager
Blake Manufacturing Co.
519 West 36th Street
New York, NY 10001

Dear Mr. Caldwell:

It has been a year since my wife and I moved to the Phoenix area to live and work. We have made many friends, and would be happy living here the rest of our lives.

The work has not been as challenging for me as I would like, primarily because of organizational changes that were instituted during the period of time between when I was hired and when I started working. In spite of that, however, it has been a great year of experience for me. The opportunity to participate in successfully managing a plant of a multilocation company has added immeasurably to my capabilities, and to increased confidence in myself as a manager.

Consequently, I have made a definite decision to seek a new position elsewhere as soon as possible. I would prefer to find again a situation where I would be assigned the challenge and responsibility of General Manager of a mid-sized company. A position as Assistant General

Manager, or as Manager of Sales and/or Operations of a larger company would be given careful study.

I am enclosing my résumé for your review, with the expectation that you may have an opening with requirements that match my qualifications. If so, I would appreciate hearing from you at your convenience.

Very truly yours,

John R. Roopper

Industrial Engineer

John R. Roopper
211 East 70th Street
New York, NY 10021
(212)755-2386

Mr. Don M. Caldwell
Human Relations Manager
Blake Manufacturing Co.
519 West 36th Street
New York, NY 10001

Dear Mr. Caldwell:

Attached please find a brief résumé of my experience, which I am taking the liberty of addressing to your attention.

I am leaving my present employer at the end of this month due to a change in top management policy. I am interested in a position with your organization as Chief Industrial Engineer.

The experience that I have is well rounded, and as you will note from the résumé, covers all phases of plant operation, methods, time study, cost and production control, labor standards, job evaluation and administration.

My present employer will be very pleased to give you a full report on what I have accomplished since I joined the concern. I am now interested in doing the same thing for you, and at the same time to assume a position of responsibility where my contribution to the productivity of the company can result in mutual benefit.

332

May I suggest that an appointment, preferably after 5 o'clock or on a Saturday, be arranged? I am certain that if you will grant me the privilege of an interview to discuss your problems, that I can show you how my background and ability can help in their solution.

Your favorable consideration, and early reply, will be awaited with interest.

Very truly yours,

John R. Roopper

John R. Roopper
211 East 70th Street
New York, NY 10021
(212)755-2386

Mr. Don M. Caldwell
Human Relations Manager
Blake Manufacturing Co.
536 West 36th Street
New York, NY 10001

Dear Mr. Caldwell:

This letter, and attached résumé, is in application for a position with your company.

As to what position, that remains undecided at the moment. I have just graduated from New York University with a B.S. in Accounting and am now interested in getting a position which will enable me to get started on my career.

I have had no working experience except as noted, during the summer and Christmas vacation periods. I am perfectly willing to accept any position you have open in the office which will give me an opportunity to start training for more responsible positions in the future.

While my degree is in Accounting, I am not necessarily interested in following Accounting per se. I feel that the formal education in this field can better prepare me for general management than for any other, since accounting is the basis of all organization planning.

May I take the liberty of calling you for an appointment within the next few days? I feel certain that a personal interview will convince you of my sincerity and provide a better opportunity of discussing how I might fit into your own plans and be of service to your company.

I thank you for your consideration and look forward to meeting you.

Very truly yours,

John R. Roopper

Manufacturing Engineer

John R. Roopper
211 East 70th Street
New York, NY 10021
(212)755-2386

Mr. Don M. Caldwell
Human Relations Manager
Blake Manufacturing Co.
436 West 36th Street
New York, NY 10001

Dear Mr. Caldwell:

With the scarcity of qualified technical personnel that exists today, it is my thought that you would be interested in my qualifications as set forth in the attached résumé.

I am currently employed and my present employer will give me an excellent reference. However the company has recently been sold and the new management is transferring some of its personnel—thereby making it necessary for me to seek another connection.

The attached résumé indicates my capabilities. I am interested in making a connection with a company such as yours where I can use my talent for administration and organization, and my thorough knowledge of mechanical design and production, in producing more goods at higher quality and lower cost.

I believe that the combination of Industrial and Technical Engineering that I can offer should be of interest to any manufacturer of mass-produced items. I have the ability to visualize new products to be added to a line, to estimate their cost and their return to the company, and to then put them into design and final production.

May I suggest that a personal interview, at your convenience of course, will permit both of us to explore the possibilities of fully utilizing my experience to date in behalf of your firm?

Your reply, with the time and place of such an appointment, will be greatly appreciated.

Very truly yours,

John R. Roopper

John R. Roopper
211 East 70th Street
New York, NY 10021
(212)755-2386

Mr. Don M. Caldwell
Human Relations Manager
Blake Manufacturing Co.
436 West 36th Street
New York, NY 10001

Dear Mr. Caldwell:

Have you ever stopped to think of the value of Market Research? Perhaps you have, and perhaps your firm has been toying with the idea of having such a department set up within your own organization.

I am looking for such a firm—one which realizes that Market Research is becoming an important function of industry today and forms the basis for all scientific planning.

The enclosed résumé outlines my experience in diversified fields and in the handling of diversified problems. Such experience can now be put to work for you, if you will give me a few moments of your time to let me tell you what I have done for similar firms in your field.

As you will note, my experience has covered everything from consumer research to policy and planning, advertising and sales. I feel that I can contribute a great deal to a company desiring to establish a department of Market

Research. I have formed departments of this type, hired and trained my own personnel, and produced results.

In numerous instances I have saved management from making mistakes such as increasing prices in a declining market, promoting new products in the face of buying reluctance, or utilizing the wrong advertising or sales approach.

May I have an interview to discuss your problems and how my experience may be of assistance? I feel certain that such an appointment will prove mutually beneficial

Your reply and favorable consideration will be awaited with great interest.

Very truly yours,

John R. Roopper

John R. Roopper
211 East 70th Street
New York, NY 10021
(212)755-2386

Mr. Don M. Caldwell
Human Relations Manager
Blake Manufacturing Co.
436 West 36th Street
New York, NY 10001

Dear Mr. Caldwell:

I am interested in a position as Office Manager with a progressive company that will make full use of my accounting education and experience, my knowledge of systems, methods and forms design, and of my ability to direct and supervise.

My present position is of this nature but does not permit any further advancement since my superior is only two years older than I am.

The attached résumé will briefly point up my knowledge of the above-mentioned functions. There is much more to tell, however, that could not be put on paper and that will indicate just how I might assist the company in many of its internal problems.

I am primarily interested in Office Management rather than straight accounting, as I feel that this offers more of a challenge than does routine figure handling.

May I call you for an appointment in the near future. I am certain that ten minutes of your time will be of mutual benefit, and that I can convince you of my suitability as a member of your staff.

Thanking you for your consideration.

Very truly yours,

John R. Roopper

Personnel Director

John R. Roopper
211 East 70th Street
New York, NY 10021
(212)755-2386

Mr. Don M. Caldwell
Human Relations Manager
Blake Manufacturing Co.
436 West 36th Street
New York, NY 10001

Dear Mr. Caldwell:

Personnel testing and selection, as you are undoubtedly aware, is becoming a very important function of a Personnel Department.

May I suggest that you read the enclosed résumé with a view toward determining if my background in this, and in related personnel work, can be of assistance to you? I am interested in a position with a company which has a progressive personnel policy. The position might be that of Personnel Director, or as an assistant in personnel, providing there is an opportunity for advancement.

My career to date has been planned along lines that will eventually lead to a top management spot in Personnel. Starting right from college, where I majored in psychology, I joined one of the largest textile mills in the country and progressed through their ranks to the position of Divisional Personnel Manager. The attached résumé outlines my functions and duties.

342

Desiring, however, to get a broader knowledge of diversified fields, I left and joined a firm of management consultants, but after a year and a half of traveling about 90% of the time, it has brought up problems—I have two small children—that can be solved only by leaving.

I would greatly appreciate the opportunity of meeting you and discussing my experience in the light of your policy, and showing you how I can be of assistance.

May I hear from you within the next few days?

Very truly yours,

John R. Roopper

John R. Roopper
211 East 70th Street
New York, NY 10021
(212)755-2386

Mr. Don M. Caldwell
Human Relations Manager
Blake Manufacturing Co.
436 West 36th Street
New York, NY 10001

Dear Mr. Caldwell:

I am presently employed as Assistant Director of Purchasing for Jones and Jones, Inc., the largest firm of naval architects in the East. I have been with the firm since 19 . . . and have an outstanding record of achievement.

As you are undoubtedly aware, my firm has suffered from serious naval-contract cancellations and, as a result, is forced to curtail the activities of my department. It is because of this that I am contacting you relative to the possibility of joining your organization.

As you will note from the attached résumé, I have a technical education, and approximately twelve years experience in purchasing and technical engineering. This experience has stood me in good stead since most of my work has been of a highly technical nature.

For five years, I had complete responsibility in purchasing over $1,000,000 worth of equipment and material daily, contacting vendors, negotiating bids, hiring and training my own personnel and working with several shipyards on the East, Gulf and West coasts.

During this period, in spite of shortages and the usual red tape, my shipyards never failed to meet schedules because of lack of material and equipment or late deliveries.

Realizing that letters and résumés are not an entirely satisfactory way of judging a person's ability and personality, may I suggest that a personal interview would be in order—at your convenience of course?

A reply setting up an appointment for such an interview is awaited with great interest.

Very truly yours,

John R. Roopper

Sales Corporate Executive

John R. Roopper
211 East 70th Street
New York, NY 10021
(212)755-2386

Mr. Don M. Caldwell
Human Relations Manager
Blake Manufacturing Co.
436 West 36th Street
New York, NY 10001

Dear Mr. Caldwell:

The attached résumé outlines my career, which has been carefully planned in the sales field. Starting immediately after graduating from college, I entered the field as a trainee and have spent my entire career as a merchandising salesman.

I believe that a salesman should be more than an "order taker"—he should have the interest of his accounts at heart and try to devise ways and means of helping them sell the goods he sells them. In that way more goods are sold by both parties. That is, I think, the secret of my success to date.

I am now interested in making a change to a company such as yours where, while starting as a salesman, I will have the chance of moving into sales administration when the opportunity presents. In the past I have built up a good sales record. I believe that with your products I can increase your sales in any given territory by merchandising rather than "order taking."

May I suggest that an appointment for a personal discussion will convince you that I can adequately represent your line? I look forward to hearing from you at an early date.

Very truly yours,

John R. Roopper

John R. Roopper
211 East 70th Street
New York, NY 10021
(212)755-2386

Mr. Don M. Caldwell
Human Relations Manager
Blake Manufacturing Co.
436 West 36th Street
New York, NY 10001

Dear Mr. Caldwell:

While the Traffic Manager's basic responsibility is to select the cheapest and fastest routing for shipments, he must also have in mind the overall operation of his employer's business.

In my case, while working for a large, nationally known food manufacturer I have, in addition to my regular duties:

Saved $200,000 a year in freight charges by recommending the relocation of warehouses in places where rates are more favorable for shipment to our thousands of customers.

Saved thousands of dollars by preventing the establishment of freight rates that would adversely affect the company.

I am a practitioner before the Interstate Commerce Commission, and have appeared before it and various state regulatory bodies.

348

In a profession where the personal element is extremely important, I can state with all due modesty that I am well known throughout the Eastern, Central and Southern states.

Attached is a résumé outlining my experience, which I believe will be of interest to you. I would like, however, to supplement it with a personal interview. If you will drop me a line suggesting an appointment at your convenience, I feel certain that I can convince you of the value of my services to an organization such as yours.

Very truly yours,

John R. Roopper

John R. Roopper
211 East 70th Street
New York, NY 10021
(212)755-2386

Mr. Don M. Caldwell
Human Relations Manager
Blake Manufacturing Co.
436 West 36th Street
New York, NY 10001

Dear Mr. Caldwell:

Having spent my entire career in the field of Training, I naturally feel that this phase of industry is extremely important. Indeed, only a few weeks ago I read an article which stressed the fact that industry is rapidly realizing that it should place more emphasis on this phase of their operations.

The attached résumé shows my experience to date—including all forms of training such as Management Development, Office and Shop Training and Supervisory programs. These I have developed, prepared the material for and given to thousands of people in the past few years.

I am now seeking another position because I feel that further opportunity is limited with my present employer—in fact, due to serious cutbacks in their government contract work, we have drastically reduced the personnel force, thereby eliminating the need for training.

May I point out, however, that a company such as yours, working on staple products, and whose sales are fairly constant, can use a person like myself, who can train your present employees in ways and means of improving their efficiency, production and morale, and who, in turn, can greatly increase your profits.

The attached résumé only highlights my accomplishments. Much more could be brought out in a personal interview, and I shall look forward to talking with you in person, at your convenience, in the near future.

Very truly yours,

John R. Roopper

12

Letters of Recommendation

Their Importance

Letters of recommendation should be part of all your job-seeking efforts. The purpose is to provide your prospective employer with additional information about you, especially as to the kind of person you are—your character and personality. Hence, good letters of recommendation should all be from those who know you and will speak well of you, except relatives: from friends, former instructors, former employers, former coworkers.

Sometimes the person who interviews you for a job will ask only for the names of one or two people as references, and sometimes you will be asked for a letter or two of recommendation. In either case, the opinions expressed by those who give you a recommendation can be the pivotal points on which your interviewer may base a decision as to whether or not you get the job you are applying for.

If you are using just a name as a reference, permission to use it should be obtained in advance. If your references are in the form of letters (whether written by you and submitted for signature, or written by the reference), each letter should be properly signed and contain the address and/or telephone number, so that your interviewer will know that the letter is bona fide and the person who signed it can be reached conveniently.

In the course of preparing your résumé, in whatever form, you can decide how and from whom you can obtain letters of recommendation, or who will give you permission to use their names as references. This information about references can be useful in applying for credit, as well as in trying to find a job or in changing positions.

In this busy workaday world, one can't always be sure that the person you have given as reference will follow through. He (or she) may be too busy to reply to an inquiry about you, or may just neglect to do so or have other reasons for not cooperating. In anticipation of such an unfavorable situation, the following procedure is suggested: Write your letter(s) of recommendation yourself, and then submit it for signature to your reference. Each letter should be different and each should mention those characteristics about you with which the person who is signing is familiar.

To give an example: The manager or foreman where you work (or have worked) knows your qualifications as a worker and the kind of duties you performed. Or your pastor or priest or rabbi may know you as a civic-minded person who undertakes civic or welfare activities voluntarily. The letters from them for which you request a signature should mention these activities, as should a letter from an executive of your chamber of commerce or your bank whom you might know, or who might know you.

Each letter of your portfolio should be short, to the point and should stress a different aspect of your personality and your work abilities. The signer should be told that the letter was written to save his or her time, and that any changes or suggestions would be welcome.

The following is a representative list of people to approach. There may be others, whose references should be in your favor. You would do well to obtain as many letters of reference as possible, even though you may not use them all:

(1) Personnel Director or executive under whom you worked.
(2) Foreman of your work.
(3) A teacher, or a professor from a technical institute, a vocational school, or a college.
(4) A librarian of your company or of your community library who knows you have done research and like to read.
(5) A member of the police department. If the applicant lives in a large city, a character reference from the precinct's sergeant would be important.
(6) A professional person—your doctor, dentist or lawyer.
(7) Several businessmen, if possible.
(8) The proper official, if you belong to a chamber of commerce.
(9) A responsible executive of a social club or welfare organization to which you belong.
(10) The family doctor.
(11) Your bank officer. (You don't need to mention the total of your account.)

These letters should not be dated too far back. Their importance cannot be overstated, since they help to give your prospective employer a chance to know you through personal testimony. Bear in mind that signed copies of all letters should be kept, and those who signed the letters should also have copies.

Some employers are impressed by membership in technical organizations, country clubs or fraternal organizations, or by church activities. Hence, if you can obtain letters of recommendation from those who are engaged in such activities or are members of such organizations, it would certainly add to the importance of your credentials.

Samples of Typical Letters of Recommendation

Recommendation from Coworker

Johnson Chemical Corp.
316 Peachtree Blvd.
Atlanta, GA 30309
(404)787-6598

To Whom It May Concern:

I believe that a salesman should be more than an "order taker"—he should have the interest of his accounts at heart and should try to devise ways and means of helping them sell the goods he sells them. In that way more goods are sold by both parties. That is, I think, the secret of Henry M. Jackson's success to date.

As Sales Manager I have worked closely with Mr. Jackson and have observed his ability to perform his job for the benefit of the company. Now that he has decided to resign his job, I will be the first to miss him at work, and the first to recommend him highly as a gentleman and as an excellent salesman.

Yours very truly,

John R. Brown
Director of Sales

This letter:
(a) expresses the applicant's qualifications as seen by his coworkers;
(b) recognizes the excellent performance of his duties.

Recommendation from Personnel Department

Johnson Chemical Corp.
316 Peachtree Blvd.
Atlanta, GA 30309
(404)695-3745

To Whom It May Concern:

Henry L. Jackson has been employed by this company for more than three years. I can recommend him enthusiastically as an intelligent man, a good worker and a man who has a bright future ahead of him in this field. He has performed his work to the complete satisfaction of his immediate supervisor.

I have no hesitation in saying that Mr. Jackson will be a credit to the company that employs him. He will doubtless explain his reasons for leaving during your interview with him. We are very sorry to see him go and wish him well in all his endeavors.

Sincerely yours,

James H. Blake
Assistant Personnel
Manager

This letter:
(a) demonstrates the worker's reliability, enthusiasm and ability;

358

(b) shows the respect that he enjoys from former employer;
(c) indicates that he would do well to continue in his chosen field;
(d) shows he is the type of worker that should be interviewed and not just passed by.

Recommendation from Foreman or Supervising Executive

Johnson Chemical Corp.
316 Peachtree Blvd.
Atlanta, GA 30309
(404)695-3745

To Whom It May Concern:

I am very glad to recommend Mr. Henry L. Jackson, whose work I supervised for two and a half years.

His work consisted in conducting chemical and physical tests in the laboratory and in making qualitative and quantitative analyses of materials for such purposes as development of new products, materials and processing methods, and maintenance of health and safety standards. He also took care of the laboratory equipment in preparation for chemical and physical tests.

I personally consider Mr. Jackson an excellent worker—a man who has been an active participant in all our tests. It is my belief that his work record and his desire to perform his duties place him an above-average employee; I do not, therefore, hesitate to recommend him very highly.

Sincerely yours,

William L. Boaz
Supervisor

This letter:
- (a) demonstrates the applicant's reliability, his willingness to assume responsibilities, and to perform his duties and cooperate with his coworkers;
- (b) attests to his dependability and knowledge of his duties in the work assigned to him.

Recommendation from Librarian

Johnson Public Library
514 Kennedy Blvd.
Newark, NJ 07104
(201)389-0439

To Whom It May Concern:

Henry L. Jackson has been a member of this library for more than ten years, as shown on his borrower's card.

During that time he has demonstrated a sustained interest in reading, and his choice of books indicates that he has an above-average intelligence. He has also made maximum use of our facilities when doing important research for projects of the company he works for. His behavior while using our facilities has always been exemplary.

Very truly yours,

Susan Demetri
Librarian

This letter:
(a) demonstrates the applicant's ability to use library facilities for independent research;
(b) shows intellectual curiosity on part of applicant.

Recommendation from Police Sergeant

Atlanta Police Bureau
175 Decatur St., S.E.
Atlanta, GA 30303
(404)715-3826

To Whom It May Concern:

Mr. Henry L. Jackson has been a resident of Atlanta for the past ten years. As sergeant of the precinct in which he lives, I have come to know him personally and can testify to the fact that he is a law-abiding citizen who shows respect for people and property.

It is a pleasure to recommend this fine man for your consideration.

Very truly yours,

George H. Wilson
Sergeant

This letter:
(a) establishes that this man has no police record;
(b) shows him to be a responsible individual, capable of asking for help from the police department—a very high recommendation;
(c) shows that he has respect for the police and thinks of them as a vital part of the community.

Recommendation from Banker

Bankers Fidelity Trust Co.
2045 Peachtree Rd., NW.
Atlanta, GA 30309
(404)657-5645

To Whom It May Concern:

I have been the loan manager of this bank for several years. Among those with whom I have had to work out loans and mortgages is Mr. Henry L. Jackson. Today, I am very proud to recommend him to you as an outstanding businessman, who is very responsible in his business obligations and devoted to his work.

I have found him to be reliable, capable of making decisions for himself, and not afraid to ask for help and advice when needed.

His sincerity in his relationship to the bank and to his financial obligations has won him the respect that he well deserves. He is worthy of your consideration, and I am certain he will be an asset to your organization.

Cordially yours,

Margaret Jones
Manager, Loan Department

This letter:
(a) establishes the man's reliability as to his obligations and his work;
(b) creates an impression of a fine business executive who takes his work seriously.

364

Recommendation from Community-Club Leader

Atlanta Community Center
22 Butler St., N.E.
Atlanta, GA 30303
(404)765-8937

To Whom It May Concern:

Henry L. Jackson has been a member of the Atlanta Community Center for the past six years.

During that time, I have had an opportunity to observe him in relation to other people. I am very happy to say that he has consistently shown himself to be a man of fine character. He has a sense of honesty and integrity and is willing to accept responsibility.

Mr. Jackson has also demonstrated qualities of leadership and has been imaginative in helping to develop community programs that maintain the interest of the boys and girls of our community.

Sincerely yours,

Joseph P. Brown
Director

This letter:
(a) indicates community spirit and a sense of civic obligation;
(b) points out qualities of leadership and initiative.

William M. Hines, M.D.
1230 W. Peachtree, N.W.
Atlanta, GA 30309
(404)654-2367

To Whom It May Concern:

I have known the Jackson family several years. My close association with them as friend and physician has enabled me to observe Henry L. Jackson closely.

I am more than happy to recommend him as a fine man, healthy in mind and body. He has an excellent reputation in our community and is well liked by everyone.

Any help you are able to give Mr. Jackson will be greatly appreciated. He is worthy as a man and as a worker.

Very truly yours,

William M. Hines, M.D.

This letter:
(a) establishes the applicant's physical and mental health;
(b) describes his fine neighborhood reputation.

Recommendation from Church of Applicant's Denomination

St. Paul Church
41 Bradley St., S.E.
Atlanta, GA 30312
(404)675-9832

To Whom It May Concern:

The Jackson family has been part of my congregation for a number of years. They attend services regularly and participate in the activities of our church. Their devotion and spiritual integrity have helped to make the performance of my duties a pleasure.

Henry L. Jackson is one of the members in charge of our Young People's Club. He can always be counted on to accept and carry out responsibilities, and he has the respect and liking of our entire congregation.

It is my sincere belief that Mr. Jackson will prove to be a fine worker. His personality, faith, friendliness and real liking for people should take him far. I am delighted to know that he is anxious to improve his occupational prospects and income, and any efforts on his behalf will be very much appreciated by all the members of this congregation.

Yours very truly,

John R. Sanfield
Pastor

This letter:

(a) shows that the applicant comes from a fine religious family, and applies the teachings of his church to his work;

(b) indicates that he has met with the approval of his minister, who joins in the congregation's high opinion of him.

13

The Interview

Preparing for the Interview

Now that you have secured an appointment, you can begin preparing for the interview. It may turn out to be a milestone in your career.

You might, if you need help, consider talking with one of the state employment service interviewers, who is qualified to discuss your qualifications in relation to the forthcoming meeting with your prospective employer. The state employment service interviewer might even notice a mannerism, or something else, that needs to be corrected, or might prove helpful in some other respect.

Research. If the appointment for the interview was made on a Monday, to take place on the coming Friday, use the intervening time to learn as much about your prospective employer's business as you can. Go to the library and look them up in a directory. Learn about their assets, their specialties, their annual gross business and the names of the top officers.

Try to read the trade publications in the field the company operates in—whether construction, engineering, electrical, retailing, food, pharmaceuticals, and so on. One or two issues of a trade publication can give you a good idea of the trends in the particular field, and build up the sort of background that can serve to give you confidence when you are actually at the interview, so that you won't feel alien to the questions that might be asked.

Transportation. Always allow a half hour more than you actually need to reach your destination. If you arrive too early, you can walk around. If your prospective employer's office is distant from your home, check directions for how to get there. Should you be driving, find out the shortest route. If you have any doubt as to the directions, call the personnel director for detailed instructions. Write them down, so that you won't get lost and arrive late for your interview.

If you go by train or plane, check the current time table. Many suburban lines change schedules frequently, especially during the summer. If flying, make your reservations in advance, and plan to be at the airport in ample time. Avoid traveling during holidays and weekends.

Most important of all, try to arrive for your interview on time; otherwise you can create an unfavorable impression of yourself. If you foresee an emergency, such as the need for a postponement, you might have handy the name of the individual you are to see, the company name, their address and telephone number.

Getting Your Material Together. As you are getting ready to start out for your interview, place at least three more copies of your résumé into your briefcase. This is in case the interviewer asks for another copy, in addition to the one you had submitted beforehand.

If you have any written samples of your work, such

370

as an annual report, or copies of blueprints, or sketches you made, or newspaper clippings about yourself and your work, take them along, after you have had duplicates made.

Appearance. Wear clothing that will make a favorable impression—stylish, but in good taste. Incline toward the conservative in dress, until you have had an opportunity to know more about this aspect of your employment opportunity. Also, wear what is suitable to the weather and the occasion. Be sure your dress or suit is clean, and not wrinkled or spotted. A woman should see that her hair is well brushed and combed and that her nails are clean and groomed. A man should also be well groomed as to hair and nails.

Personal Contact. Once you appear at the reception desk, greet the receptionist cordially and announce your name: "I'm Mortimer Hirsch and I have a 10:30 appointment with Mr. George Fielding."

Assume an air of confidence when greeting Mr. Fielding. In speaking with him stay within the purpose of your interview. Don't go off on tangents and speak of matters that are not relevant, and try not to be overawed by the elegant office or the impressive personality of your interviewer. Speak clearly. Avoid such clichés as "I couldn't care less," which is really quite meaningless.

Keep in mind that the interviewer's main purpose is to find someone who will be an asset to the company he represents. And don't bring up the matter of salary, hours, benefits or vacations until the job has been offered to you. Most likely, these matters will be taken care of when the decision to place you on the payroll has been made.

If you are asked to fill out an application blank, furnish references or take a physical examination, cheerfully indicate your willingness to comply.

When the interview is over, make your farewell pleasant and courteous, and leave promptly. Also give a friendly nod to the receptionist on your way out.

"Dos and Don'ts" for the Interview

This checklist will help you with your interview:

(1) Take with you a summary of your past experience and education, with names, places, and dates. A complete résumé is better, if you have one.

(2) Have ready a list of three to six people or firms (with names, addresses and telephone numbers) who may be used as references.

(3) Take your Social Security Number with you.

(4) Do not take anyone with you to the interview.

(5) Be on time for your interview, not even one minute late.

(6) Dress well—cleanly and neatly. If you are a woman, do not use flashy makeup or excessive jewelry. If you are a man, avoid sports clothes.

(7) Even if you feel tired or not too well, sit up and look alert. Do not yawn, slouch or show signs of nervousness.

(8) Do not smoke or chew gum.

(9) Answer all the employer's questions frankly, honestly and briefly. Do not boast, but speak with confidence.

(10) If you are asked to fill out a number of forms or take various tests, do so as cheerfully and as efficiently as you can.

(11) When you are asked, point out the value of your past experience, especially as it applies to the job you are seeking, and do it with confidence.

(12) Do not argue with the person interviewing you.

(13) Do not criticize others—including your past employers or associates—or apologize for your lack of experience.

(14) Keep your personal, domestic or financial problems out of the conversation. The employer only wants to know what you can do and how well you can do it. He is not interested in your personal troubles.

(15) Be polite. Show courtesy and respect for the person interviewing you. If the employer offers suggestions about other jobs or types of work, but will not hire you for the one you are applying for, listen to what he has to say. He may provide you with just the lead or advice you need to secure another job.

(16) Do not be arrogant.

If you feel you were not able to give a good impression on your first interview because you were nervous or for other reasons, do not let it worry you. Your experience on that occasion will help you handle the next one better.

The Interview for the Executive, the Professional, the Office Worker

Let us assume your job campaign has produced one or more interviews. As you start out for these interviews, bear in mind that each person who has requested or suggested an interview is doubtless very busy. Therefore, make it a point to *be on time*. You'll be starting off on the wrong foot if you are late for the interview. It's a fact that many executives regard punctuality as a virtue that an employee must have.

Sometimes it is the policy of a company to have applicants fill out certain forms prior to the interview. *Do this willingly and graciously.* Remember that the interview starts the moment you step in from the front door—the receptionist, the personnel assistant, even a guard, will be aware of your reactions as their first impression of you.

Some companies—and their number is increasing—insist on giving applicants psychological tests of different kinds, depending on the position under consideration. Some applicants regard these tests as a necessary evil, while others are afraid of them.

It is suggested that you take the tests in your stride—very likely you will come out quite well from them. If, however, you try to be oversmart about taking them, you will not be as likely to make the grade. Some executives think the tests are a waste of time; others regard them as an excellent corollary to the overall impression and record they have of the applicant and, therefore, as very helpful.

Remember that the interviewer, whether a personnel assistant or the president of the company, is interested in matching your qualifications with the position that is open. He knows the specifications—you do not. Do not, therefore, try to dominate the interview or show how interesting a conversationalist you can be. Answer questions briefly but fully. Don't forget that a good salesman knows *when to stop talking*. In other words, take your cue from the interviewer, answer his questions, but don't expound at length, and *don't argue over a difference of opinion.*

Sit quietly, be relaxed and don't fidget. If you show signs of nervousness or peculiar mannerisms, the interviewer may decide that you are a person who will cause friction or unrest among coworkers. This does not, however, mean that you should maintain a cold or distant exterior. You certainly should show some enthusiasm for and interest in the position you are applying for. Above all, *don't smoke* unless it is suggested. And *don't chew gum*. Many people object to it and regard it as impolite.

Watch your language. Profanity, off-color jokes and uncouth gestures, as attempts to show how relaxed and friendly you feel, do not appeal to any interviewer. Avoid them.

Some General Suggestions:

Try not to forget that the purpose of the interview is to find out *what you can do for the company*. Don't, therefore, try to sell yourself on the basis of needing a job, supporting a family or wanting more money. Talk about what you can do to best serve the company by means of the job you are applying for.

Prepare yourself before the interview. Find out all you can about the company, its officers, its products, its methods of operation, its problems, etc. If you can, you might secure a Dun & Bradstreet report on the company.

In a sense, you are trying to make a sale—to sell yourself and your abilities—at the interview. For this reason it is important to take your cue from the interviewer and leave when the interview is obviously over. Do not stay on and keep talking, trying to emphasize what has already been said. A good salesman leaves on his own initiative and thereby leaves the customer with a desire for more information. Remember, if the interviewer suggests another interview, you have gone a long way toward getting the job you are after.

And—very important—*be sure to send a note of thanks* for the interesting discussion. You might also, in your note of thanks, say something about the points that were discussed.

The more important the position, the more interviews you will probably have with different officials of the company. We have seen applicants lose out because they grew impatient and tried to press for a decision. We have seen others who grew disgusted and resisted additional interviews. Needless to say, these attitudes did not "make the sale."

Now let us assume you have "made the sale." You have reached the point where the matter of remuneration is to be discussed. Don't bring this matter up yourself. Let the employer make the overture. The chances are that you will be asked the compensation you would consider. *This is the most crucial moment in the entire interview*. If you price yourself too high, or too low, you are taking a chance.

Generally speaking, as regards an executive or supervisory position, other factors such as bonuses, pension, group insurance, etc., are to be considered in connection with remuneration. It is recommended that the remuneration figure you submit should be from 10 to 15 percent higher than what you expect will be offered. If the employer accepts your figure, you are that much ahead. If the employer indicates that your figure is not in line with his, you can always make it lower, considering the other factors mentioned above.

Of course, each interview is different. Each will present different problems that will require different solutions. The points we have mentioned here are basic and should serve you well if you follow them.

Typical Questions Asked at the Executive, Professional and Office-Worker Interview

Following are typical questions that you will doubtless be asked at the interview. They should be studied, and the answers practiced:

Do I have your résumé?

Do you think you are qualified for this type of work?

Do you know that the position you are applying for has the following duties?

Why do you want to work for us?

Did you bring your references with you?

Are we free to call these references for a personal, direct answer?

Why did you leave your last position?

Can you tell me some more about your experience?

The salary for your type of position is 15 percent less than that specified in your résumé. Why?

Is your present employer aware of the fact that you wish to leave?

Have you ever been fired from a job?

Do you enjoy the work you are now doing?

Have you had education beyond college?

What were your average grades in college?

Why do you feel that you have the qualifications for this position?

What duties did you like the most in your past jobs?

What kind of people do you like most as coworkers?

What made you leave your last position?

What do you consider the greatest accomplishment in the business world?

Can I see the portfolio of your references?
Can I see the history of your salaries?
What is the lowest salary you will accept?
What other organizations, besides the ones you
   described in the résumé, do you belong to?
Are you willing to relocate?
How much of your time can you devote to travel, in
   case of need?
What type of reading, besides newspapers, do you
   do?
How often do you watch television?
What kind of programs do you enjoy most on
   television?
Are you undertaking any additional adult educa-
   tion? What field? Why?
How much do you enjoy sports?
Have you collected unemployment insurance at
   any time?
How long, within the last three years, have you
   been sick?
How often do you take a physical examination?
Do you have any objection to some overtime,
   occasionally?
What kind of security clearance do you have?

Typical "Thank-You Letters" after the Interview

Henry L. Jackson
211 East 70th Street
New York, NY 10021
(212)765-7898

Mr. Peter Jones
Gray Electronic Co.
125 Barclay Street
New York, NY 10008

Dear Mr. Jones:

Thank you very much for the interview you granted me after the referral from the World Personnel Service.

Attached please find the complete résumé you suggested.

If you wish further information or would like me to come for another interview, please let me know.

Sincerely yours,

Henry L. Jackson

Henry L. Jackson
211 East 70th Street
New York, NY 10021
(212)765-7898

Mr. William Blackwell
Electronic Components Corp.
610 West 19th Street
New York, NY 10011

Dear Mr. Blackwell:

Please accept my thanks for the courtesy extended to me in granting yesterday's interview.

I was very much impressed with the information you gave me about the company. I hope, therefore, that after you have read my résumé, you will come to a favorable decision, as I certainly would like to be part of your staff.

Please feel free to check all my references. Should you need additional information I shall be glad to supply it. May I look forward to hearing from you?

Sincerely yours,

Henry L. Jackson

Henry L. Jackson
211 East 70th Street
New York, NY 10021
(212)765-7898

Mr. Ralph G. Harrison
Carbondale Manufacturing Co.
2 Washington Street
New York, NY 10003

Dear Mr. Harrison:

It was a pleasure to meet you and to learn about your fine organization and its management.

I am very sorry indeed that I must decline your offer of a position with your firm at this time. The difference between the salary I stipulated in my interview and the salary you offered makes it all but impossible for me to accept your offer, much as I would like to work for you and your company.

Should you think that we might have further discussion in regard to the matter of salary, please do not hesitate to telephone me for an appointment.

Very truly yours,

Henry L. Jackson

The Interview for the Skilled and Semiskilled Worker

In this type of interview, the worker is asked the kind of work he is looking for and how he can match his experience to the job for which he is applying.

Despite a job description, the duties of each job are likely to vary with each employer, because of the size of the company, its geographic location and other factors. Some jobs require the worker to specialize in certain tasks. In other jobs, the worker is required to undertake a whole range of tasks. Of course, job duties keep changing as technology advances and new industrial processes are developed, and as new products or services are offered.

The matter of salary will doubtless come up for discussion during the interview. This is something that the worker himself must decide, after considering such matters as the kind of business, whether some of the so-called fringe benefits are sufficient to compensate for some sacrifice in salary, the union scale (if there is a union), the physical conditions where the work is to be performed, whether the job is indoors or outdoors, its possible hazards, and whether it requires standing, stooping or heavy lifting. Full consideration of these and other job-related factors should bring about a satisfactory evaluation of the salary. In some instances the company pays standard hourly rates.

Typical Questions Asked at the Skilled- and Semiskilled-Worker Interview

What can I do for you?
Why are you interested in working for us?
What are your personal qualifications?

What is your experience?

Do you want to be paid by the hour or by the week?

What experience do you have in this field?

Is this job in line with your experience?

What makes you think you can fill the requirements of this job?

Have you served in the armed forces?

What kind of work did you do in the Army?

Are you wondering if this job is worked in shifts?

Do you know that the opening we have is in the 4:00 to 12:00 P.M. shift?

Are you a union man?

Why did you leave your previous job?

Have you ever been fired from a job? Why?

Can I see your references?

How long have you known Mr. . . .?

Are you familiar with our method of payment?

Are you willing to join the union with which we have a contract?

Who recommended you to us?

Are you a Communist?

Do you have any prejudices about working with members of minorities?

Are you able to work overtime in case it is necessary?

Are you a religious person?

Is it all right to check your references?

14

Women in the
Labor Force

The Growing Importance of Women in the Labor Force

Employment of women and minorities is increasing in many fields: in communications, in administration and in various professional, nonprofessional and business areas. In fact, the trend is toward open and equal hiring in all occupational areas. Some fields, such as public relations and advertising, have in the past been more open to women in executive as well as in nonexecutive or nonadministrative posts. On the other hand, men have predominated in editorial positions on larger newspapers and periodicals. However, more women are now entering these fields too. They are even entering the business press, long a male stronghold, at an increasing rate.

Engineering and some of the sciences have also been male occupations traditionally. A recent study of U.S. women who entered the science and engineering fields showed that they were less likely than their male colleagues to strive for advanced degrees. They were more likely to work for the government, to be out of the labor force at times, and to work part-time or part-year. Where women are paid less than men, they are just as likely to remain with their employers as men are; but in the sciences they are less likely than men to have written something for publication.

Women college graduates have been inclined to think that careers in medicine and engineering are too demanding and too likely to require full-time commitment. Up to now, women have considered engineering unfeminine and requiring abilities that women do not usually possess. Also, they have tended toward higher degrees in areas where they felt they could contribute most, rather than in the scientific and engineering fields. On the whole women have preferred part-time schedules and flexible hours.

Today, the picture is rapidly changing, as women acquire a broader understanding of the opportunities open to them in the sciences and in engineering. They have been receiving better guidance as to job opportunities, and are finding that they fit very well into these professions.

Our technological and industrial society needs men and women who possess the necessary specialized knowledge and skill. Heretofore, the exclusion of women—whether through custom, role stereotyping or discrimination—from the scientific and technical fields has seriously affected their aspirations toward equality.

Women who aspire to become doctors make the decision to study medicine rather early in life. They generally come from elite or professional families, and are most often graduates of private colleges, relying on parents for their financial support. Single women are subject to certain stresses, not so much for financial reasons, but rather because of academic demands. For those who marry, child-bearing may intermittently interfere with their studies or careers. On the whole, the strain between career and family is somewhat resolved when they begin to practice as doctors.

Except in times of crisis, very little effort has been made in the United States to interest women in the medical field. To accommodate women in medical schools, the schedule of studies should be made more flexible to allow for part-time attendance, and more attention should be given to the establishment of day-care facilities for the care of the children of women medical students who are mothers.

Careers in management and administration are also open to women today. The stereotype of the submissive woman's role is fast disappearing as more and more women are undertaking jobs that require leadership and executive ability. The phenomenon of women in upper management positions is bound to have a salutary effect on hiring and upgrading women employees at all levels, and in eliminating discrimination. Intramural and extramural training programs for women should be established to implement the new attitude toward the role of women in business and the professions.

In the areas of community and government, volunteer organizations should use women in more meaningful roles. Counseling and placement services for women should be expanded.

On a national scale, women with less educational background are more likely to work in atypical jobs than women who are better educated. This is particularly true of white women. Attitudes and other noneducational factors have been found to have relatively little effect on the matter of atypical jobs for women who are less equipped.

A great deal of attention has been given as to women

in skilled blue-collar jobs, though progress in that direction has not been as rapid as might be desired. During the Second World War, close to three million women undertook blue-collar jobs. With the end of the war, most women were gradually phased out of these jobs. During the 1960s, however, the number of women in such jobs increased by about 80 percent; and vocational and trade school enrollments among women also expanded.

National Apprenticeship Information officers have indicated that women are very able to pass the tests for apprenticeships. Advocates of employment opportunities for women are giving increasing attention to job structuring, grading and classification in the hiring and promotion of women employees.

Expanding Opportunities for Women in the Labor Force

The hours of work for women are expected to remain stable, with the average working week likely to drop by less than 0.1 percent a year; that is, from 38.1 to 37.8 hours for nonfarm workers. The decrease in working hours would be negligible were it not for an expected influx of part-time workers eager to supplement the family income.

Among those young people who are likely to have "copped-out" of work during the late 1970s, it is not likely to have been the women. It is estimated that the birthrate will continue to decline and that women will be entering the labor force in increasing numbers.

Dislocations. About 34 million young workers will have entered the labor force during the 1980s. They are the result of the upsurge in the birthrate that occurred following the Second World War. However, the current decline in the birthrate will have its effect relating to specific groups as follows:

Teenagers. The slowdown in their rate of growth in the labor force may improve job opportunities for those who will compete in an anticipated expanding economy.

Young workers. Projected changes may mean keen competition among workers in their twenties for entry-level jobs, but will offer better opportunities for advancement to higher levels, especially where the number of competent older workers may be lessening.

Older workers. The surge of young workers may increase the pressure on older workers to retire sooner than otherwise planned. In any case, the trend toward earlier retirement is expected to continue. It will very likely lead to greater emphasis on preretirement planning and the development of community-service projects for which retired workers could contribute paid or volunteer part-time work.

Black workers. The 33 percent increase expected in the black labor force between 1968 and 1985 will raise the total number of black workers to 12 million by the latter date. Since an upward occupational trend is dependent, in part, upon improved job qualifications, the current educational progress among blacks promises to bring about better occupational opportunities.

The continuing increase of women in the labor force, particularly young women in their child-bearing years, will result in the establishment of more day-care centers for the children of such working mothers.

Certain job requirements may need to be adjusted to deal with the physical characteristics of women.

As more and more married women enter the labor force, the additional family income they contribute may change the patterns of consumption and the living styles of families. More services may be required to replace those performed by the housewife, and expenditures for leisure-time activities may have to be reckoned with.

The Increasing Number of Women in the Labor Force

The not quite 37 million women in the civilian labor force are a cross section of all the women in the nation. They comprise all ages from 16 to 70 or more, and represent every race and color. They include the married, the never-married, the widowed, the divorced or separated; and they live on farms, in suburbs, and in central cities.

In the last decade women accounted for almost three-fifths of the increase in the civilian labor force. They have supplied many of the necessary workers for expanding industries—particularly the service industries, in which they have made important contributions to the functioning of such vital areas as health and education. Women also continue to provide a worthy labor resource in the goods-producing industries, and are now entering into occupations of a less traditional nature. Let us categorize the areas in which women are contributing in increasing numbers:

In the 1970s, 46 percent of all women 16 years of age and over were in the labor force—a considerably higher percentage than the 34 percent which prevailed twenty-five years earlier. Although women are more likely to be working during their younger years, or if they have no children or have recently completed their schooling (between 18 and 24), their overall rate of participation is relatively high and is consistent (about 55 percent) with the so-called prime working years between 25 and 54 years of age. In fact, the greatest gains in the labor-force rates since 1950 have been among women in the 20 to 54 age group.

About one out of seven women workers is employed in a blue-collar job, as compared with half of the men in this category. Women are about as likely as men to be operatives, but very seldom are they employed as skilled craft workers—the occupation for one out of five men. Only about 5 percent of all craft workers are women.

As to service workers, more than one out of five are women, but only one out of eleven are men. Eight out of ten women, and virtually all men service workers, are employed in occupations other than private household work.

Women from minority groups are less likely than white women to hold white-collar jobs (44 percent compared with 63 percent). The former are more likely to be in service work (37 percent compared with 20 percent) or blue-collar work (18 and 14 percent, respectively). The proportion of women from minority groups who are employed in clerical work has continued to increase, reaching 25 percent in the 1970s. At the same time, the proportion in private-household work has continued to decline, dropping to 11 percent. A decade ago these figures were 12 percent and 30 percent for clerical work and private-household work, respectively.

Increases in employment opportunities for women would depend largely upon a continued improvement in general economic conditions. During 1974 and early in 1975 during the economic recession, the unemployment rate for women, as well as that for men, rose steadily, reaching a post-Second World War high. It has been ascribed to the fact that many businesses were forced to restrict hiring, and resorted to layoffs to deal with the economic slowdown.

As the economy continued to recover, the upward trend in employment has been especially favorable for women. Women are increasingly enjoying opportunities in selected professional and technical, managerial, clerical, skilled-crafts and service occupations. Then, too, legislation prohibiting sex discrimination in employment is continuing to open new opportunities for women to train for and enter into more diversified jobs and to advance to jobs requiring higher levels of skill and specialization. Women should keep informed about opportunities before deciding on careers, so that they may be able to use this information in entering fields where skilled workers are in demand.

In addition to new job opportunities that expanding occupations offer, women now have greater opportunities in specialized education. These, together with the advantage of greater longevity among women, and the trend toward smaller families, will be factors in the increasing opportunities for women in the labor force.

Such factors as age, marital and family status, education, race or ethnic background and—if she is married—the husband's income, are factors in a woman's relationship to the labor force. However, nine out of ten women will, at some time in their lives, be part of the labor force.

Typically, a woman enters the labor force after she has finished her schooling. Then she works for a few years before she marries and has her first child. A very small proportion of women leave the labor force permanently at this early period. For those married women who continue to work, most experience some breaks in employment during their child-bearing and child-rearing years. However, an increasing proportion of young married women with or without children are remaining in the labor force.

Of the 43 million women who were not in the labor force in the 1970s, almost 35 million were keeping house, about 4 million were students, and about 4 million were out of the labor force because of ill health, disability or other reasons.

Women are more likely to be white-collar workers than men. They make up two-fifths of all professional and technical workers. Most are teachers (2.1 million) or health workers (1.4 million). In fact, women account for 72 percent of teachers (except college teachers) and 64 percent of all health workers. Women are less likely than men to be managers and administrators, and represent only about one-fifth of these workers. They comprise, however, 78 percent of all clerical workers (including more than 4 million women secretaries, stenographers and typists).

Occupations That Are in Increasing Demand for Women

A mistaken notion, and one that should be corrected, is that most women do not need to work. As evidence to the contrary, the Bureau of Labor Statistics indicates that even in prewar years, one-fifth of employed women were the principal wage earners of their families. There was an increase in this proportion with the effect of the Second World War on the male population. Today, many women would be glad to leave the labor market to be at home, if their menfolk were earning enough to maintain the household.

According to some factory managers, the volume produced by women workers in jobs formerly held by men is equal to, or even greater than, that of the men. Many plants have testified to the efficiency of women on jobs that were new to them. Despite this, however, there have been numerous reports of women being placed in blind-alley jobs where neither ability nor length of service can result in advancement. In these circumstances, women have been taken on as helpers and not as mechanic learners. In many machine shops, women don't often get beyond the helper classification. Discrimination as regards promotion is one of the major reasons why women quit factory jobs.

On the positive side, however, it has been noted that many factories have made changes in machinery and work arrangements to adapt jobs for their women workers. Cranes, hoists and other lifting devices that can be operated by women have been installed, enabling them to undertake jobs that otherwise would be too heavy for them. In one plant, steel jigs too heavy for women were replaced by masonite jigs weighing less than one-tenth the weight of the steel jigs. Another company provided women with long-handled wrenches, which require less strength than those with short handles. A very large tool company built its plant and designed its machinery expressly for their women workers. They installed machines of proper height, adjustable chairs, footrests, weight-lifting devices and electric button controls. There is a continuing trend to provide machinery and other plant equipment that can be used by women, and thus to enhance efficiency in their work. In cases where continuous work at one process has been found to be too tiring, rotation with other tasks has been arranged.

Is it logical to assume that companies that have found women very satisfactory as workers, and that have retooled large sections of their plants to accommodate them, will continue to employ women? The answer is yes. There is evidence that the need for women workers will continue in the following areas:

(1) In industries producing consumer goods, such as electrical products, shoes, textiles, jewelry and similar industries, and where women have always had opportunities for employment.
(2) In service industries, such as restaurants, laundries, households, and selling, and where work shortages will continue to be acute.
(3) In community services, such as health, welfare, social work, child care and recreation.
(4) In specialized technical and professional work, such as medicine, nutrition, education, research, communications and various scientific areas.
(5) In the manufacture of goods.
(6) In various business and clerical operations, such as clerical work, statistics, accounting and programming.
(7) In selling, buying, marketing, promotion and administrative jobs.

Here are some of the occupations in which women are in great demand and that offer excellent opportunities to them:

Accountant
Actuary
Advertising Worker
Aeronautical Engineer
Agricultural Engineer
Anesthetist

Announcer,
   Radio–Television
Anthropologist
Architect
Astronomer
Athletic Coach

Bank Officer
Biochemist
Biologist
Book Editor
Buyer (Merchandising)
Cartographer
Ceramic Engineer
Chemical Engineer
Chemist
Civil Engineer
College Placement
   Officer
College Teacher
Commercial Artist
Communications Expert
Compiler of
   International
   Information
Computer-Operating
   Personnel
Dentist
Dietitian
Draftswoman
Economist
Electrical Engineer
Electronics Engineer
Engineering Technician
Executive Secretary
Export and Import
   Assistant
Fashion Designer
FBI Special Agent
Foreign-Language Book
   Editor
Foreign-Language
   Teacher

Foreign-Market Analyst
Foreign-Service Officer
Foreign-Student
   Advisor
Forester
Fund Raiser
Geographer
Geological Engineer
Guidance Counselor
Historian
Home Economist
Hospital Administrator
Industrial Designer
Industrial Engineer
Interior Designer
Landscape Architect
Lawyer
Librarian, Professional
Market-Research
   Worker
Mathematician
Mechanical Engineer
Medical Technologist
Metallurgical Engineer
Meteorologist
Mining Engineer
Newspaper Reporter
Nurse, Registered
   Professional
Occupational Therapist
Oceanographer
Optometrist
Osteopathic Physician
Personnel Worker
Pharmacist
Physical Therapist

Physician
Policewoman
Political Scientist
Programmer, Computer
Psychologist
Publicist
Public-Relations
  Worker
Purchasing Agent
Real-Estate Broker
Recreation Worker
Rehabilitation
  Counselor
Sanitarian
Sanitary Engineer
Science Technician
Secretary
Social Worker
Sociologist
Soil Scientist
Speech Pathologist and
  Audiologist
Statistician
Surveyor
Systems Analyst
Teacher, Elementary
  School
Teacher of English for
  Foreigners
Teacher, Secondary
  School
Technical Writer
Translator, General
Translator, Scientific or
  Literary
Typist
Urban Planner (City
  Planner)
Veterinarian

This is the time to appraise your abilities, interests and experience, so as to capitalize on your personal assets. Today, you can count on an increasing appreciation of your value as a woman worker—it's the trend.